HBJ SPELLING

BLUE

Richard Madden

Thorsten Carlson

Harcourt Brace Jovanovich, Publishers
Orlando   New York   Chicago   Atlanta   Dallas

Acknowledgments

ACKNOWLEDGMENT

Handwriting models in this book are reproduced with permission of Zaner-Bloser, Inc., from the series *Creative Growth with Handwriting*, © 1975, 1979.

Graphic Concern, Inc.
Design and Production

ART CREDITS

Rick Brown: 3, 47, 86, 87, 88, 94, 95; Olivia Cole: 23, 28, 38, 39, 48, 49, 56, 70, 71, 80, 81, 98, 99, 100, 101, 104, 110, 111, 125, 133, 134, 138, 139; Jill Dubin: 11, 13, 17 (T), 27, 64, 65, 72, 83, 85, 108, 119, 124, 132; John Killgrew: 12, 16, 20, 29, 52, 122, 123, 129, 137; Jared Lee: 1, 15, 57, 62, 63, 73, 75, 126, 127 (R); Karen Loccisano: 69, 90, 92, 112, 114, 116, 120, 130, 131, 136, 141, 142, 144; Lorretta Lustig: 21, 36, 37, 46, 50, 51, 93, 96, 97, 106, 107, 117, 127 (L), 128, 135; Sal Murdocca: 4, 7, 9, 24, 34, 35, 42, 43, 54, 55, 58, 59, 82, 84, 102, 103, 115; Jan Pyk: 2, 6, 10, 14, 17 (C), 18, 21 (C), 22, 25 (C), 26, 29 (C), 44, 45, 53, 91, 109, 113, 140, 143, 145, 146, 147, 148, 149, 150, 151, 152, 153, 154, 155, 156, 157; Jerry Smath: 5, 8, 19, 25, 30, 31, 32, 33, 40, 41, 60, 61, 74, 76, 77, 89, 121; Sally Jo Vitsky: 78, 79.

PHOTO CREDITS

Cover, © Michal Heron/Monkmeyer Press Photo; pages: 66, 67, 68, 118, 135, Inbert Gruttner; 105 © David Huges/Bruce Coleman.

KEY: top (T); bottom (B); left (L); right (R); center (C)

Printed in the United States of America
ISBN 0-15-328550-8

Contents

1

Do the picture words begin with the same sound?
Color the circle if they do.

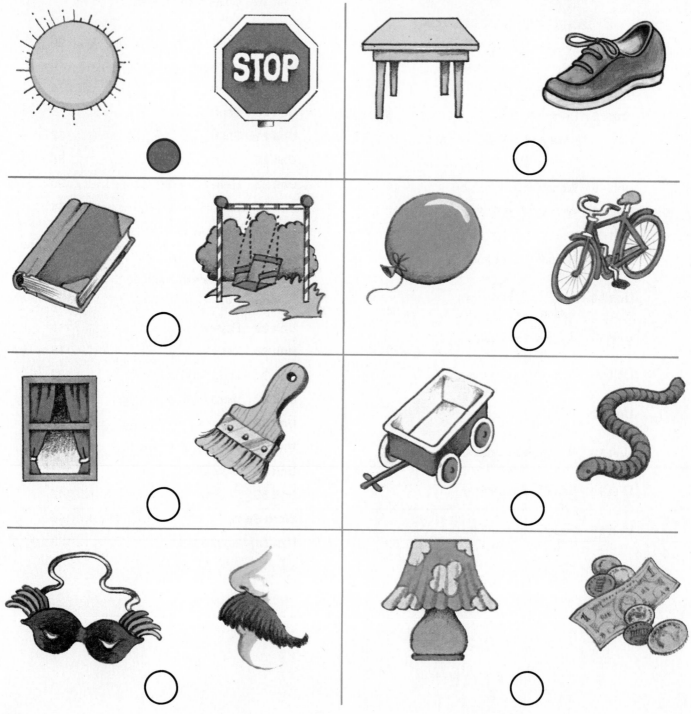

Match the beginning sounds.

girl

ring

hat

leg

red

goat

3

Say the word for the key picture.
Say the words for the other pictures.
If the word begins with the same sound,
draw a line under the picture.

dog

pig

tiger

Match the beginning sounds.

duck

pillow

moon

bus

leg

hat

Do the picture words begin with the same sound?
Color the circle if they do.

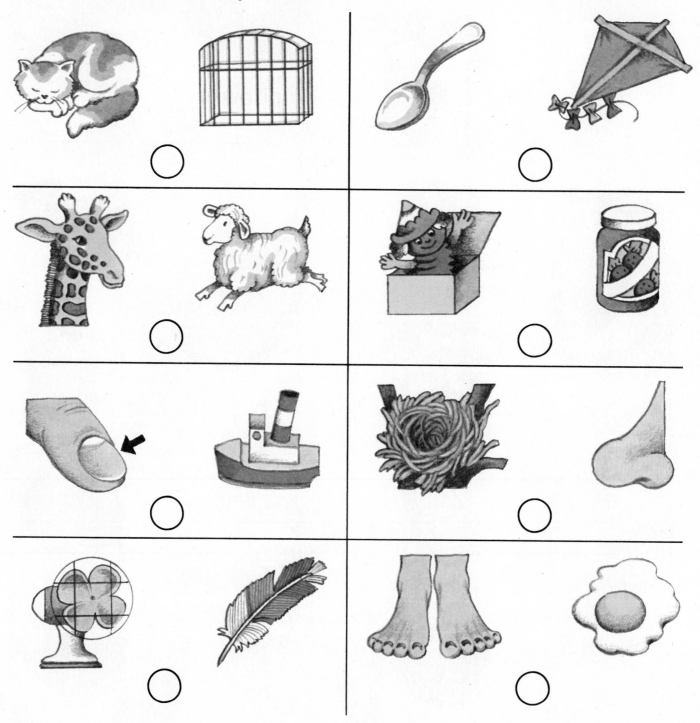

Say the word for the key picture.
Say the words for the other pictures.
If the word begins with the same sound,
draw a line under the picture.

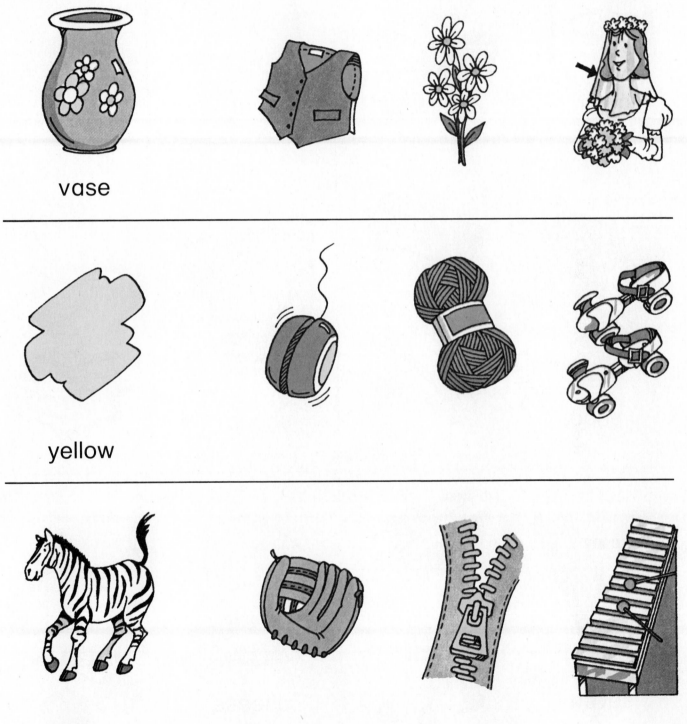

vase

yellow

zebra

Match the beginning sounds.

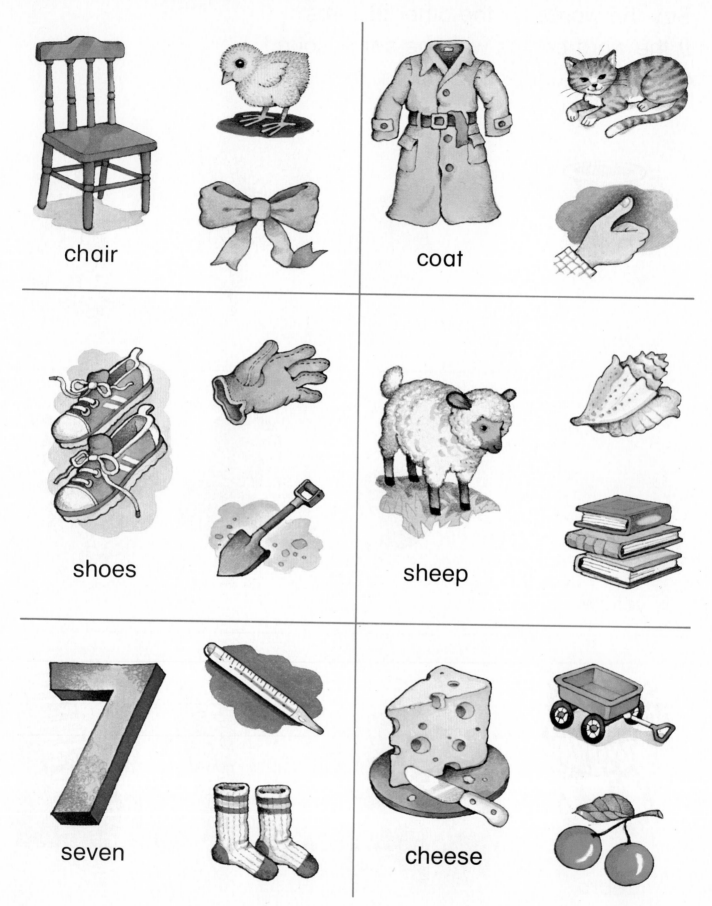

chair

coat

shoes

sheep

seven

cheese

Match the beginning sounds.

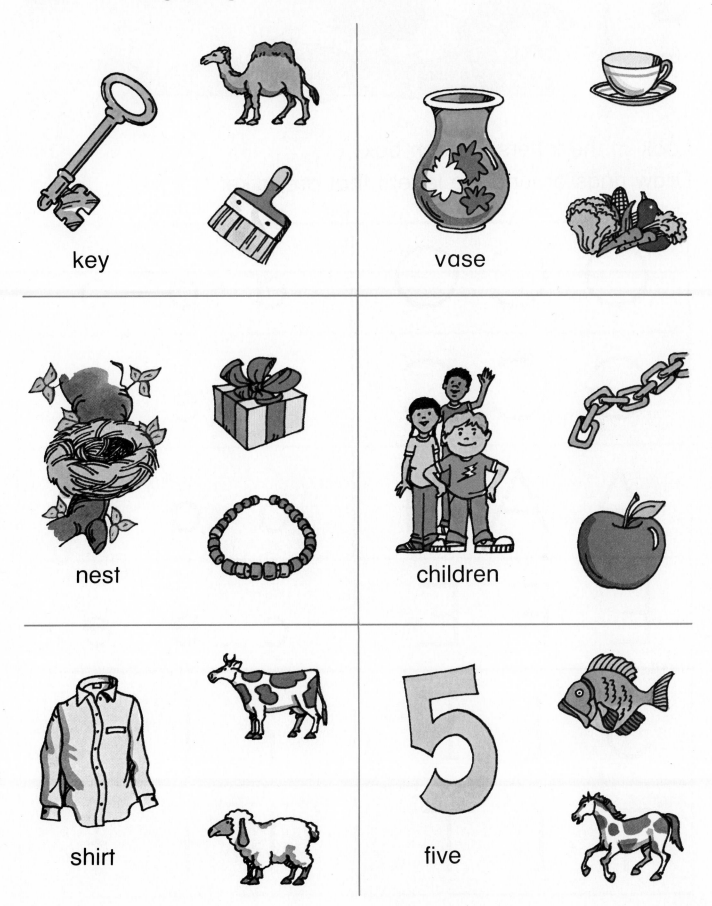

key

vase

nest

children

shirt

five

Look at the letters in each box.
Draw rings around the letters that are alike.

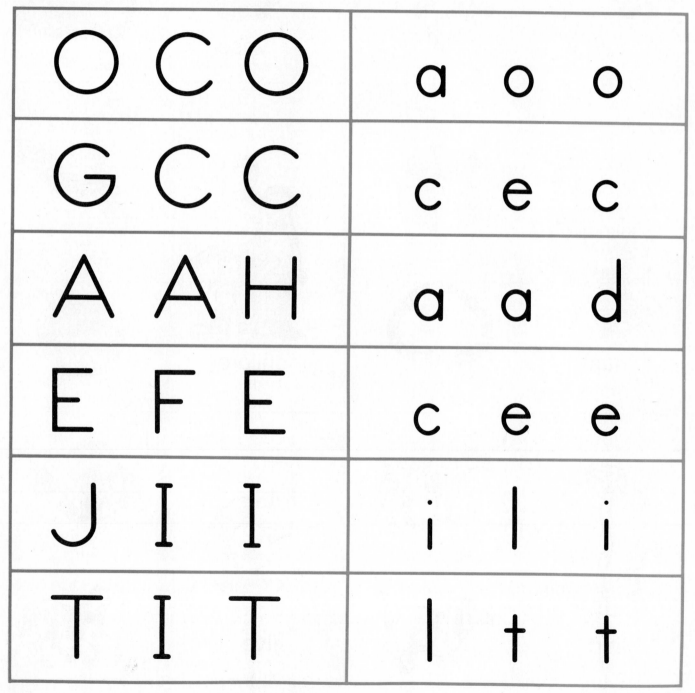

O C O	a o o
G C C	c e c
A A H	a a d
E F E	c e e
J I I	i l i
T I T	l t t

The word <u>in</u> begins with the letter **i.**

Write i and I.

The word <u>ten</u> begins with the letter **t.**

Write t and T.

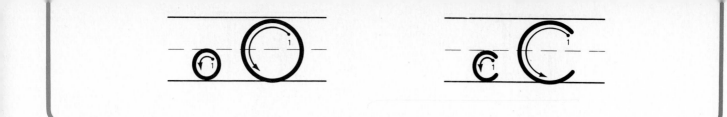

The word <u>on</u> begins with the letter **o.**

Write o and ◯ .

The word <u>cat</u> begins with the letter **c.**

Write c and C .

The word <u>apple</u> begins with the letter **a.**

Write a and A .

a

A

The word <u>egg</u> begins with the letter **e.**

Write e and E .

e

E

4

Look at the letters in each box.
Draw rings around the letters that are alike.

M W M	n m m
N N M	n h n
V U U	u u n
S Z S	s c s
R R P	r n r

u U   s S

The word <u>up</u> begins with the letter **u.**

Write u and U .

u

U

The word <u>sun</u> begins with the letter **s.**

Write s and S .

s

S

 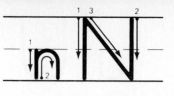

The word <u>moon</u> begins with the letter **m.**
Write m and M.

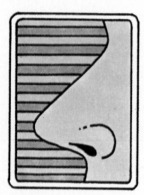

The word <u>nose</u> begins with the letter **n.**
Write n and N.

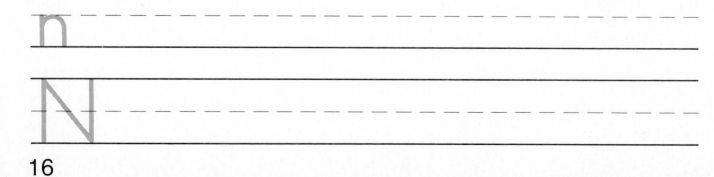

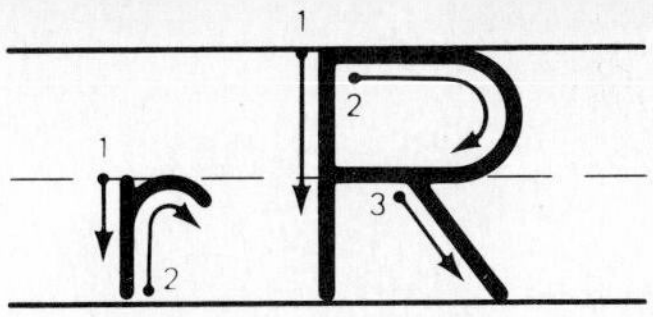

r R

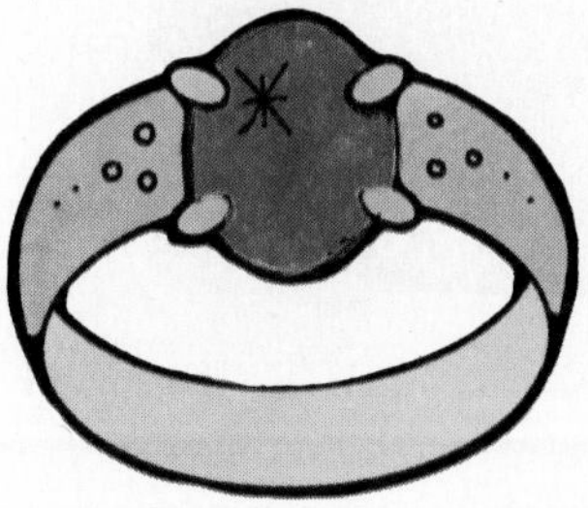

The word <u>ring</u> begins with the letter **r.**

Write r and R.

r

R

Write the letters.

rs   rn

mu   sm

ru   su

Draw rings around the letters that match
the key letters.

d D	Dubois, Idaho
h H	Homer, Ohio
f F	Alfred, Florida
b B	Banks, Alabama
l L	Loda, Illinois

d D   f F

The word <u>dog</u> begins with the letter **d.**

Write d and D.

d

D

The word <u>fan</u> begins with the letter **f.**

Write f and F.

f

F

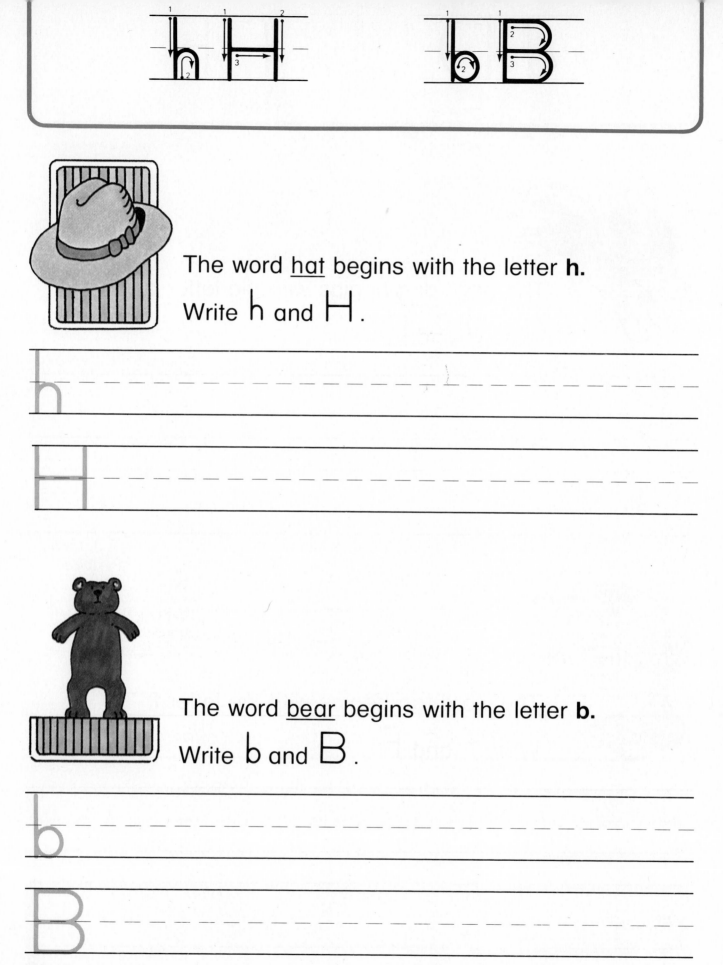

The word <u>hat</u> begins with the letter **h.**

Write h and H.

The word <u>bear</u> begins with the letter **b.**

Write b and B.

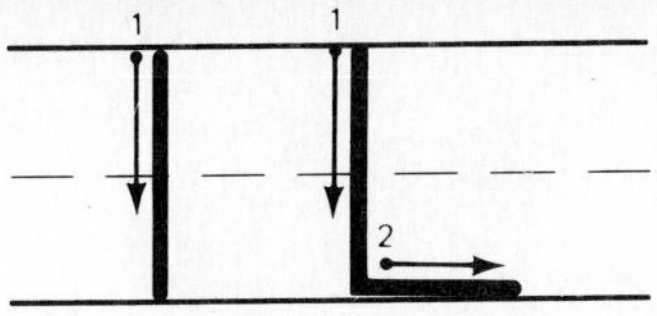

The word <u>lamp</u> begins with the letter **l**.

Write **l** and **L** .

l

L

Write the letters.

f l

b l

d e

h u

b a

d o

Draw rings around the letters that match
the key letters.

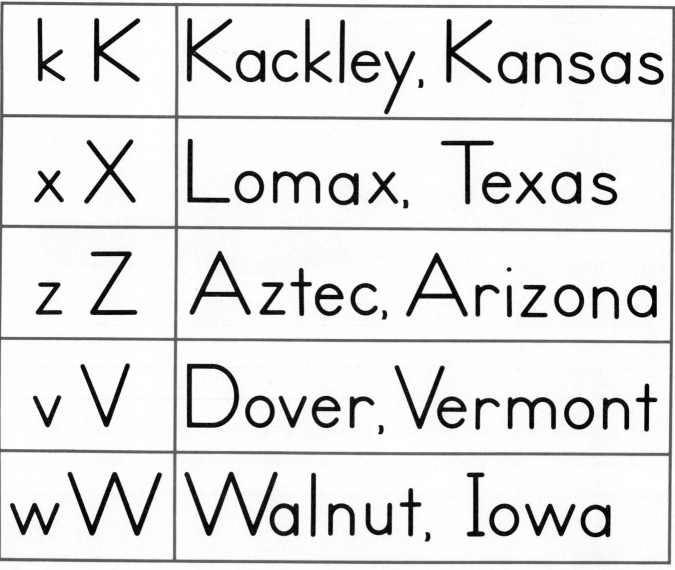

k K	Kackley, Kansas
x X	Lomax, Texas
z Z	Aztec, Arizona
v V	Dover, Vermont
w W	Walnut, Iowa

The word <u>vase</u> begins with the letter **v.**

Write v and V .

V

V

The word <u>watch</u> begins with the letter **w.**

Write w and W .

W

W

The word <u>kite</u> begins with the letter **k.**

Write k and K .

The word <u>box</u> ends with the letter **x.**

Write x and X .

Zz Z

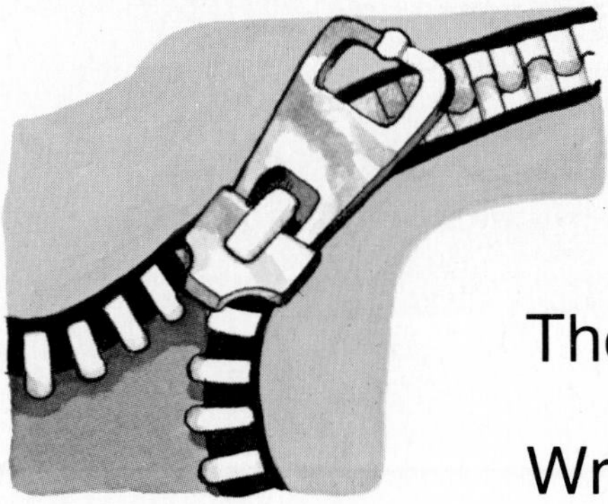

The word <u>zipper</u> begins with the letter **z.**

Write Z and Z .

z

z

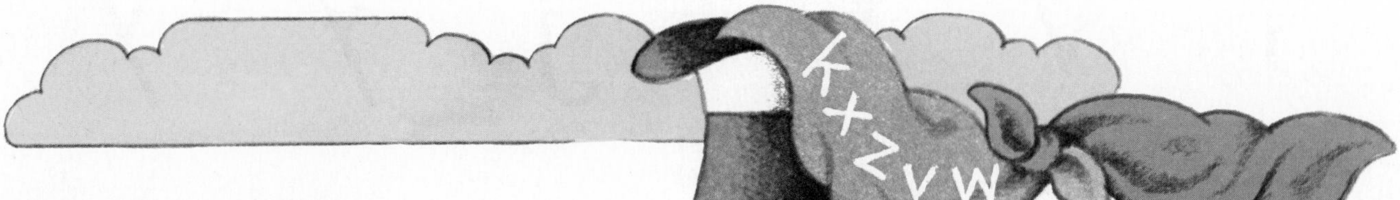

Write the letters.

wh   ve

ks   ox

ze   sw

7

Look at the letters in each box.
Draw rings around the letters that are alike.

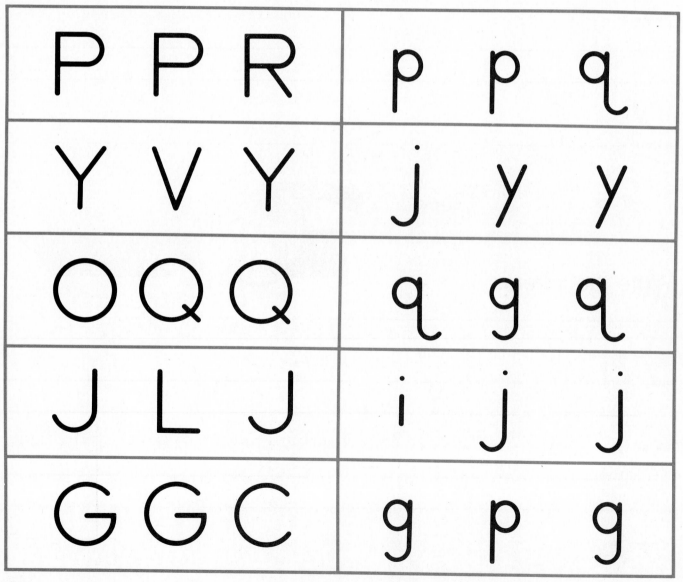

P P R	p p q
Y V Y	j y y
O Q Q	q g q
J L J	i j j
G G C	g p g

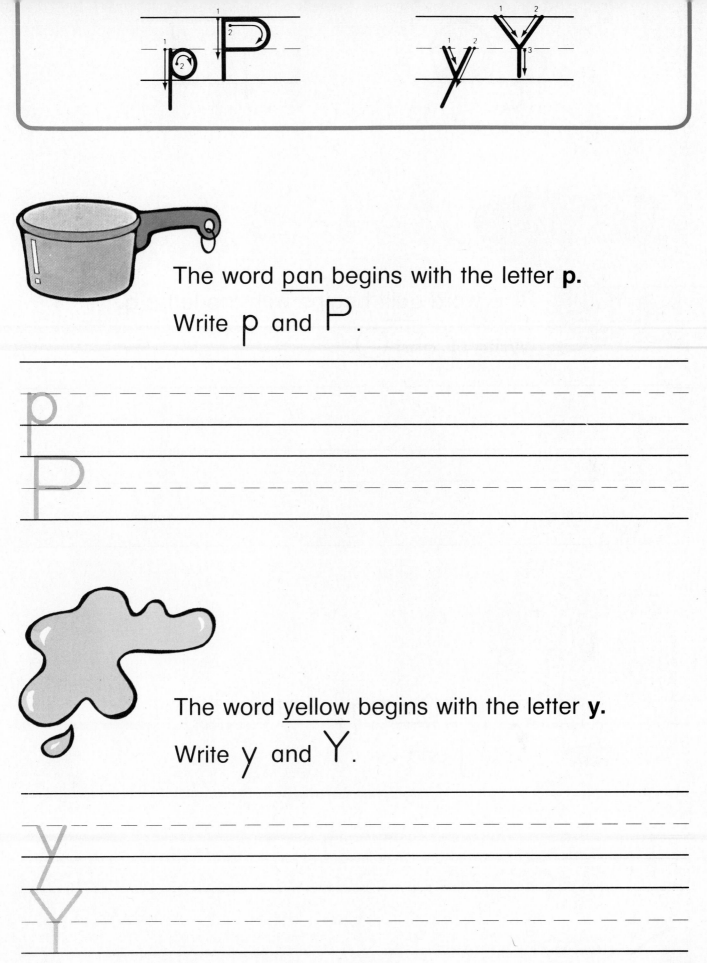

The word <u>pan</u> begins with the letter **p.**

Write p and P.

The word <u>yellow</u> begins with the letter **y.**

Write y and Y.

q Q   j J

The word <u>quilt</u> begins with the letter **q.**

Write q and Q.

The word <u>jar</u> begins with the letter **j.**

Write j and J.

g   G

The word <u>go</u> begins with the letter **g.**

Write g and G.

g

G

Write the letters.

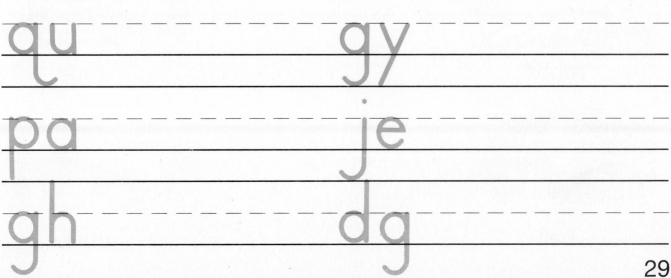

gu   gy

pa   je

gh   dg

8

Draw a line between the picture words that begin with the same sound.

bee

wagon

wolf

bear

rabbit

rope

bell

bone

30

Write the letter **b** if the picture word
begins like <u>bird</u> 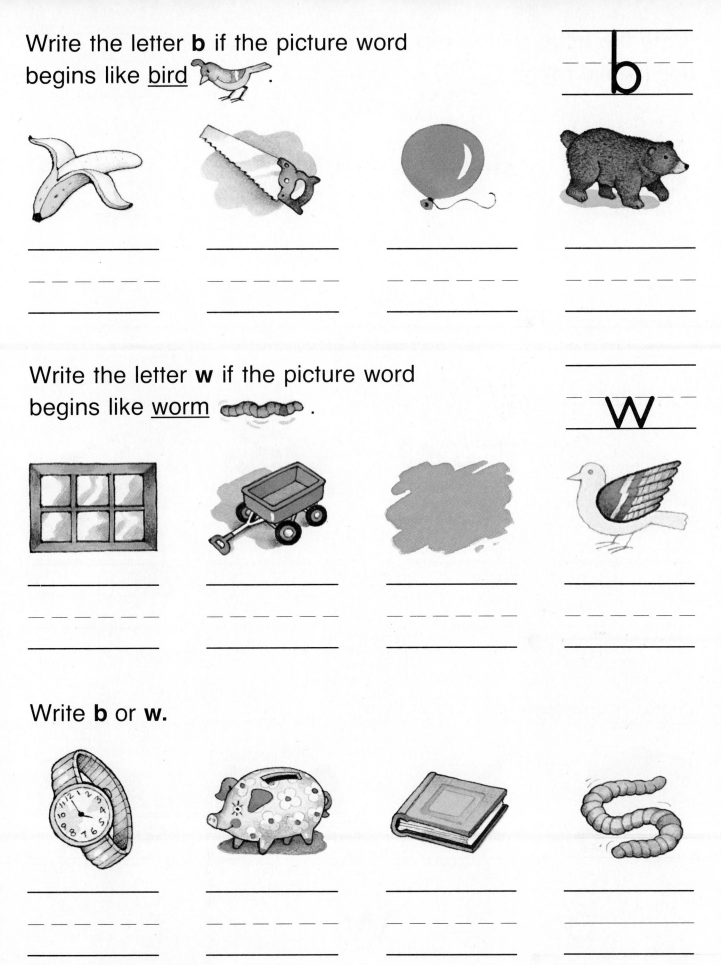 .

b

_____ _____ _____ _____

_____ _____ _____ _____

_____ _____ _____ _____

Write the letter **w** if the picture word
begins like <u>worm</u> .

w

_____ _____ _____ _____

_____ _____ _____ _____

_____ _____ _____ _____

Write **b** or **w.**

_____ _____ _____ _____

_____ _____ _____ _____

_____ _____ _____ _____

Write the letter r if the picture word begins like <u>rabbit</u> .

r

Write b or r.

Draw a line from the letter to the picture.

b   w   r

Write the beginning letter in the word.

bat

at

bib

ib

bee

ee

rock

ock

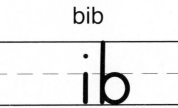

rain

ain

red

ed

web

eb

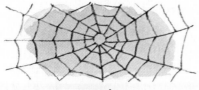

worm

orm

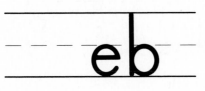

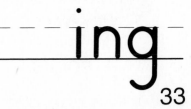

wing

ing

Listen for the beginning sound in <u>mop</u> . The letter **m** stands for that sound.

Listen for the beginning sound in <u>saw</u> . The letter **s** stands for that sound.

Draw a ring around the letter that stands for the beginning sound.

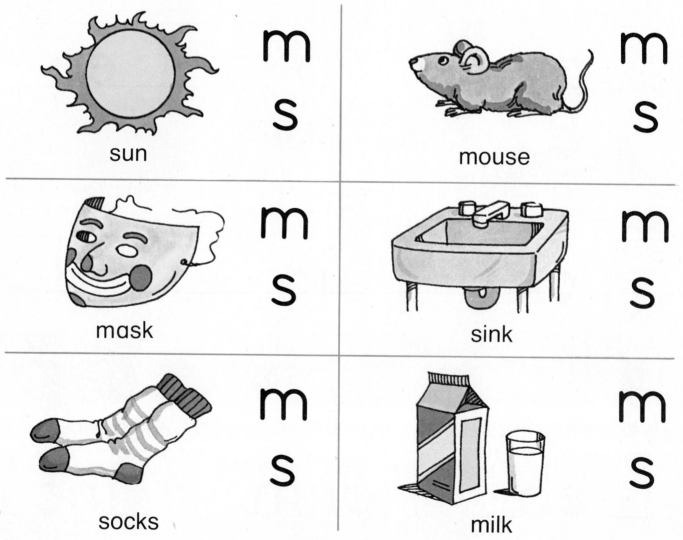

sun	m s	
mouse	m s	
mask	m s	
sink	m s	
socks	m s	
milk	m s	

Write the letter **s** if the picture word
begins like <u>saw</u> 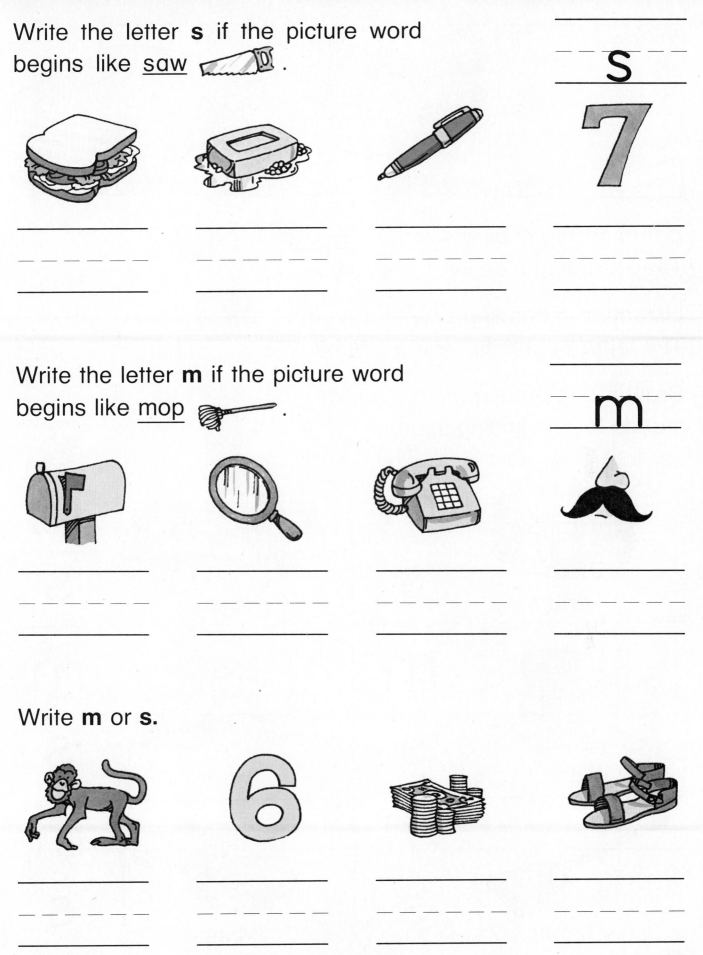 .

s

7

Write the letter **m** if the picture word
begins like <u>mop</u> .

m

Write **m** or **s**.

Listen for the ending sound in <u>bus</u> .
The letter **s** stands for that sound.

Listen for the ending sound in <u>drum</u> 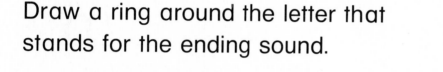.
The letter **m** stands for that sound.

Draw a ring around the letter that
stands for the ending sound.

drum	m s	
bus	m s	
gas	m s	
worm	m s	
broom	m s	
dress	m s	

Write the letter **s** if
the picture word ends like <u>bus</u>  .

Write the letter **m** if
the picture word ends like <u>drum</u> .

Write **m** or **s.**

If the picture word begins like <u>hand</u>, put an **X** on the picture.

If the picture word begins like <u>leg</u>, draw a ring around the picture.

The letter **h** stands for the beginning
sound in <u>horse</u> 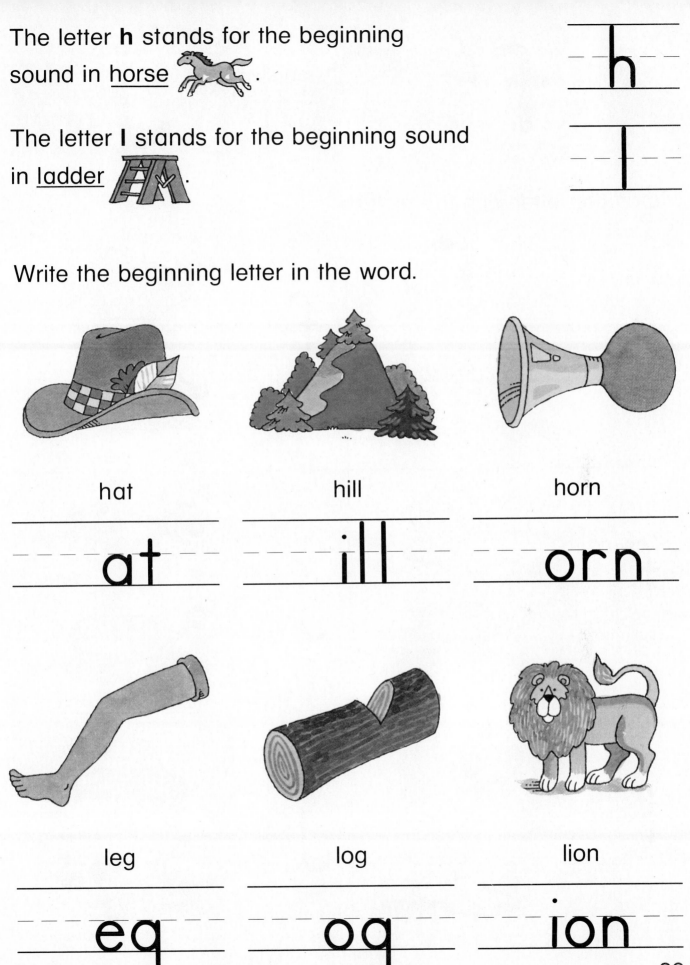.

The letter **l** stands for the beginning sound
in <u>ladder</u> .

Write the beginning letter in the word.

hat

at

hill

ill

horn

orn

leg

eg

log

og

lion

ion

Match the letter with the picture.

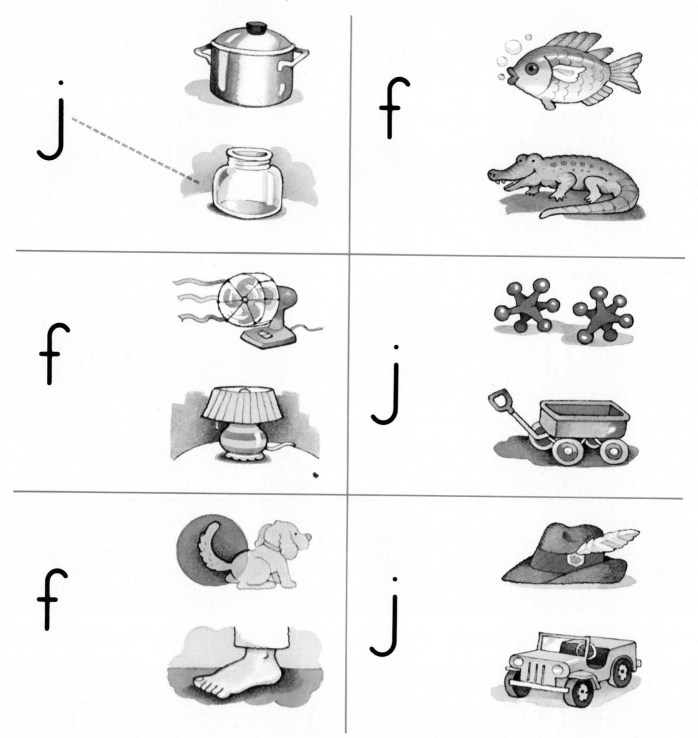

j   f

Write the letter **j**
if the word begins
like <u>j</u>ar  .

Write the letter **f**
if the word begins
like <u>f</u>ish .

_____

_____

_____

_____

_____

_____

_____

_____

Which picture words begin like <u>goat</u> ?
Draw a ring around the pictures.

g

Which picture words begin like <u>deer</u> ?
Draw a ring around the pictures.

d

Match the letter with the picture.

Write the letter **g**
if the picture word begins like <u>goat</u> .

Write the letter **d**
if the picture word begins like <u>deer</u> .

 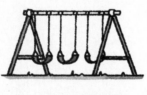 

Write **g** or **d.**

Listen for the ending sound in <u>dog</u> .
The letter **g** stands for that sound.

Listen for the ending sound in <u>red</u>  .
The letter **d** stands for that sound.

Draw a ring around the letter
that stands for the ending sound.

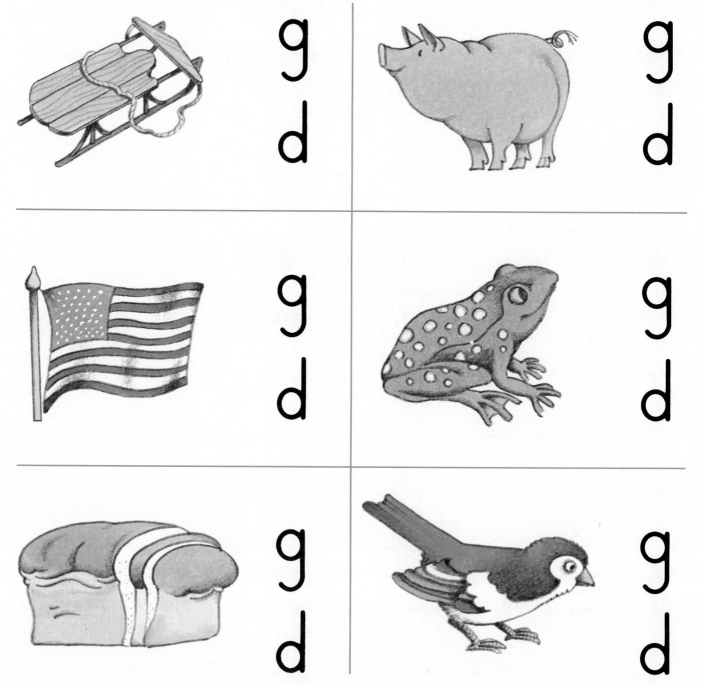

Write the letter that stands for the ending sound.

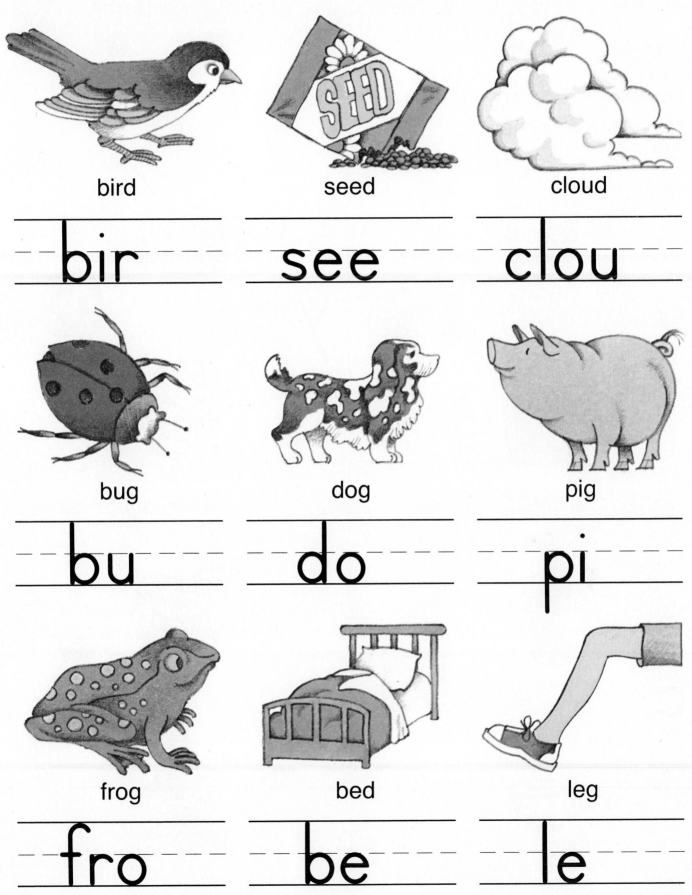

bird

bir

seed

see

cloud

clou

bug

bu

dog

do

pig

pi

frog

fro

bed

be

leg

le

45

12

Do the picture words begin with the letter?
Draw a line if they do.

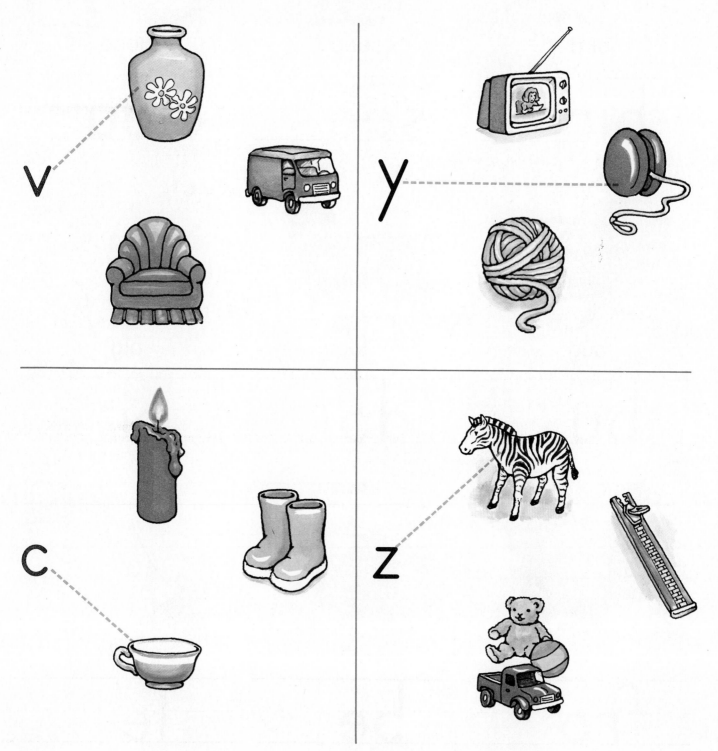

The letter **c** stands for the
beginning sound in <u>cat</u>  .

_____ c _____

The letter **z** stands for the
beginning sound in <u>zebra</u>  .

_____ z _____

Write the beginning letter in the word.

cage	corn	cow
age	orn	ow

 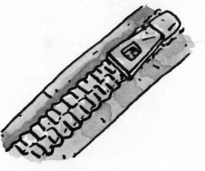

zebra	zoo	zipper
ebra	oo	ipper

47

___ ___

v   y

Write the letter **v**
if the word begins
like <u>vine</u> ____ .

Write the letter **y**
if the word begins
like <u>yellow</u> ____ .

If the picture word begins like <u>cat</u> ,
write **c** on the picture.

If the picture word begins like <u>yellow</u> ,
write **y** on the picture.

If the picture word begins like <u>vine</u> ,
write **v** on the picture.

p  t

Which picture words begin like <u>pig</u> or like <u>turtle</u> ?

Draw a line under the pictures.

p

t

p

t

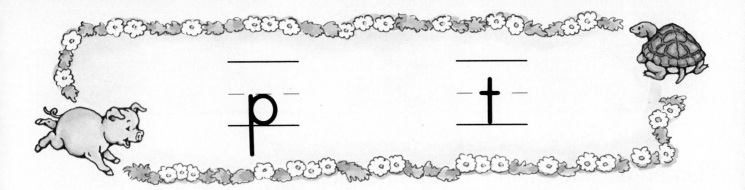

p   t

Write the first letter in the word.

pig

ig

pen

en

potato

otato

top

op

turtle

urtle

ten

en

tomato

omato

pin

in

pea

ea

Listen for the ending sound in <u>sheep</u>.
The letter **p** stands for that sound.

Listen for the ending sound in <u>spot</u>.
The letter **t** stands for that sound.

Draw a ring around the letter that
stands for the ending sound.

p
t

p
t

p
t

p
t

p
t

p
t

Write the letter that stands for the ending sound.

soap

__soa__

hop

__ho__

soup

__sou__

hat

__ha__

boat

__boa__

cat

__ca__

coat

__coa__

sheep

__shee__

cup

__cu__

53

14

Draw a line between the picture words that begin with the same sound.

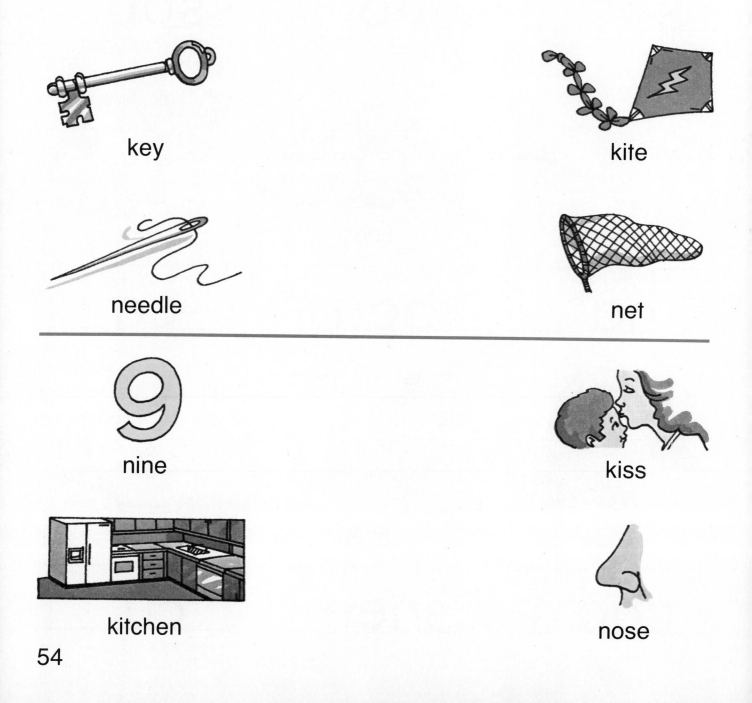

key

kite

needle

net

nine

kiss

kitchen

nose

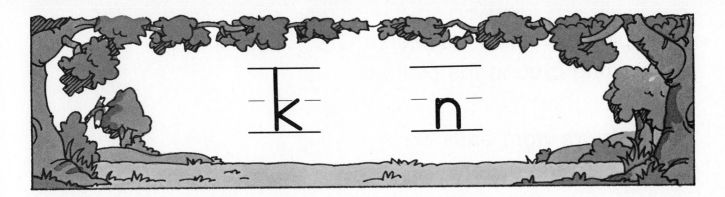

Write the first letter in the word.

key

ey

kite

ite

kiss

iss

nail

ail

nose

ose

nine

ine

kitten

itten

name

ame

nest

est

If the picture word ends like <u>sun</u> ,
draw a ring around the picture.

If the picture word ends like <u>six</u> ,
put an **X** on the picture.

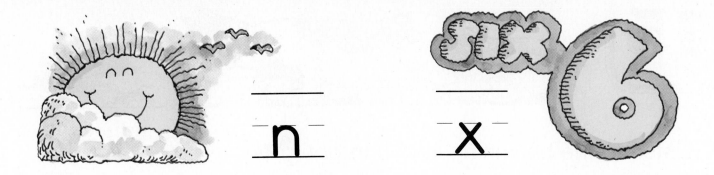

n ___ ___ x ___

Write the letter that stands for the ending sound.

___

57

15

Listen to the beginning sound in <u>ant</u>
and the middle sound in <u>cat</u> .
The letter **a** stands for that sound.

Do the picture words have **a?**
Draw a line under the ones that do.

 a

a

a

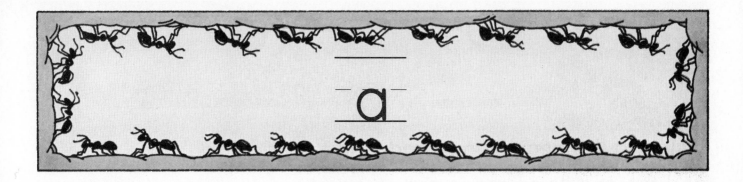

a

Write the missing letter in the word.

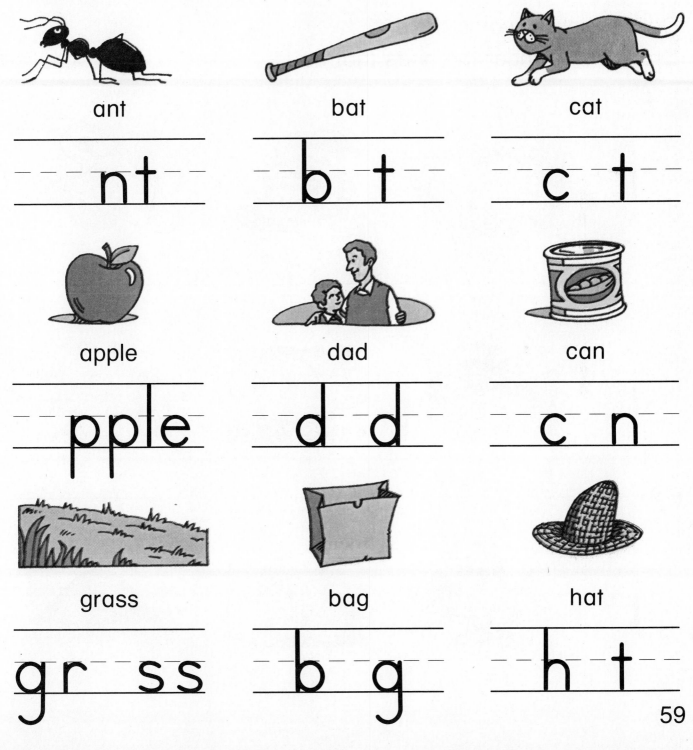

ant

＿ nt

bat

b ＿ t

cat

c ＿ t

apple

＿ pple

dad

d ＿ d

can

c ＿ n

grass

gr ＿ ss

bag

b ＿ g

hat

h ＿ t

59

Listen to the beginning sound in <u>in</u>
and the middle sound in <u>pig</u> .
The letter **i** stands for that sound.

Do the picture words have **i**?
Draw a line under the ones that do.

i |

i |

i |

i

Write the missing letter in the word.

chin

ch_n

bib

b_b

pin

p_n

ring

r_ng

six

s_x

milk

m_lk

fish

f_sh

pig

p_g

hill

h_ll

16

Listen to the beginning sound in <u>up</u>
and the middle sound in <u>bug</u>.
The letter **u** stands for the sound.

Listen to the beginning sound in <u>egg</u>
and the middle sound in <u>nest</u>.
The letter **e** stands for that sound.

Match the letter with the picture.

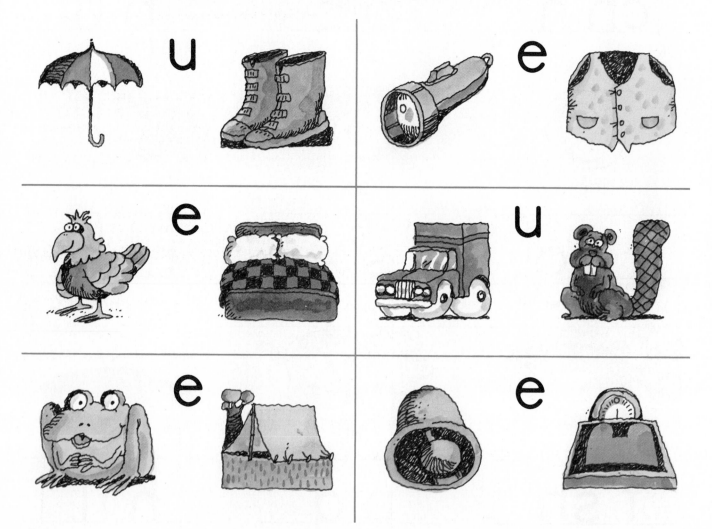

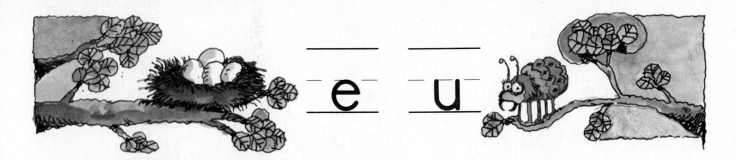

e u

Write the letter **e** or **u** in the words.

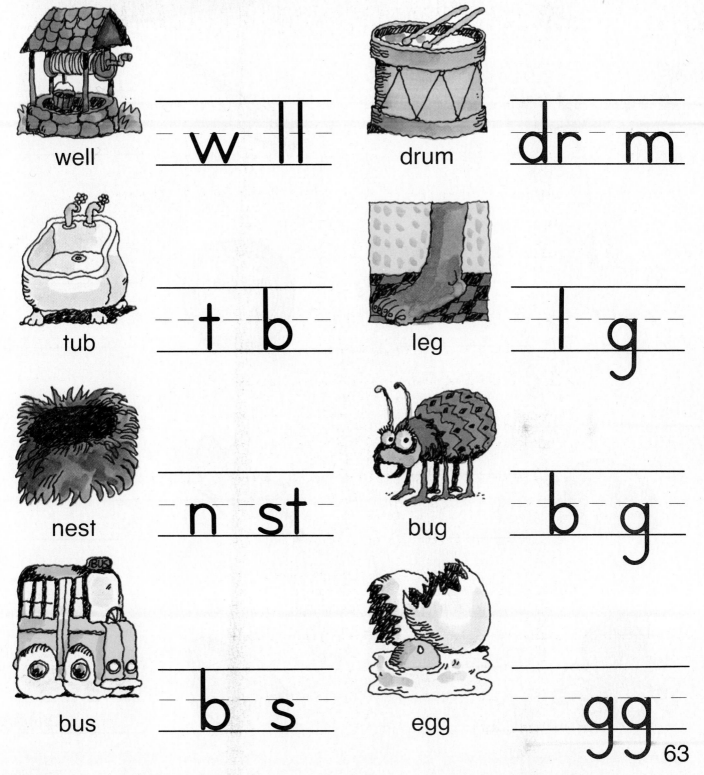

well   w ll   drum   dr m

tub   t b   leg   l g

nest   n st   bug   b g

bus   b s   egg   gg

63

Listen to the beginning sound in <u>on</u>
and the middle sound in <u>hop</u>.
The letter **o** stands for this sound.

Write **o** if the word has the same sound
as the beginning of <u>on</u>.

o

Write the letter **o** in the words.

box

b _ x

rock

r _ ck

frog

fr _ g

fox

f _ x

Write **a, e, i,** or **u.**

lips

l _ ps

cat

c _ t

drum

dr _ m

ten

t _ n

17

Say the spelling words.
Spell each word.
Write each word two times.

1. the _____ _____

2. you _____ _____

3. are _____ _____

4. I _____ _____

5. am _____ _____

6. was _____ _____

1. Write the words that sound like
the letter names.

R   U

_____   _____

- - - - - - - -   - - - - - - - -

_____   _____

2. Write the two words that begin with **a.**

_____   _____

- - - - - - - -   - - - - - - - -

_____   _____

3. Write the words that begin with these letters.

w _____   th _____

4. Write the words that end with these letters.

m _____   s _____

5. Make the sentences tell about you.
Write the beginning word.

_____

- - - -

_____ am at school.

_____

- - - -

_____ am working in my book.

Write the missing words.
Use each word once.

_____

Tim and _____ like to hide.

_____

"Where _____ you, Tim?" I said.

_____

"Are _____ behind the chair?"

_____

"Are you behind _____ TV set?"

_____

"Here I _____," said Tim.

_____

"I _____ under the table."

68

Say the words.

Finish the story.

_____

Suki _____ a pet.

_____

Her pet is a _____ .

_____

Missy and Ted _____ pets, too.

_____

But _____ have cats.

_____

They _____ all at my house today.

69

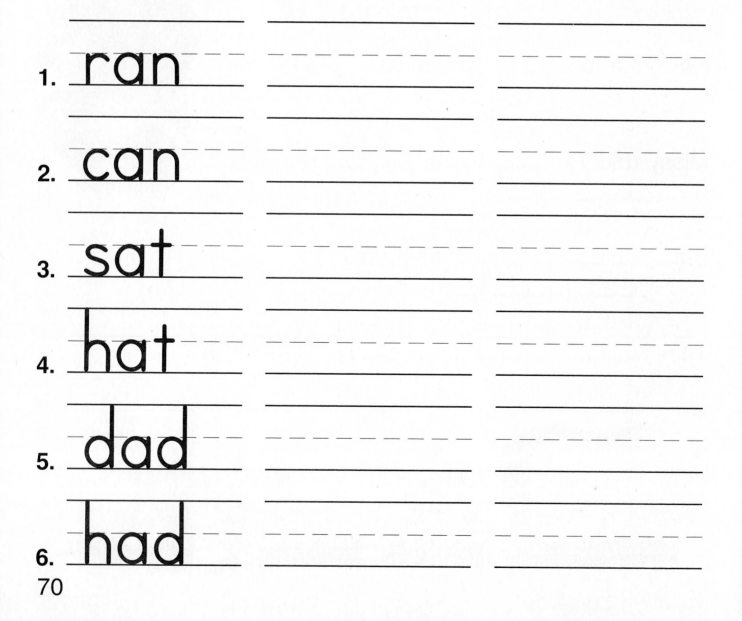

18

You spell the middle sound in <u>ran</u>
with the letter **a.** This sound is short **a.**
Say the words. Listen for the sound
of short **a.**
Write each word two times.

1. ran

2. can

3. sat

4. hat

5. dad

6. had

1. Write the two words that start with **h.**

h _____   _____

2. Write the words that end with these letters.

n _____   _____

d _____   _____

t _____   _____

3. Write the word that tells what Jack did.

Jack _____.

Jack _____.

ran

can

sat

hat

dad

had

The letters of the alphabet are in ABC order. These letters c d e are in ABC order.

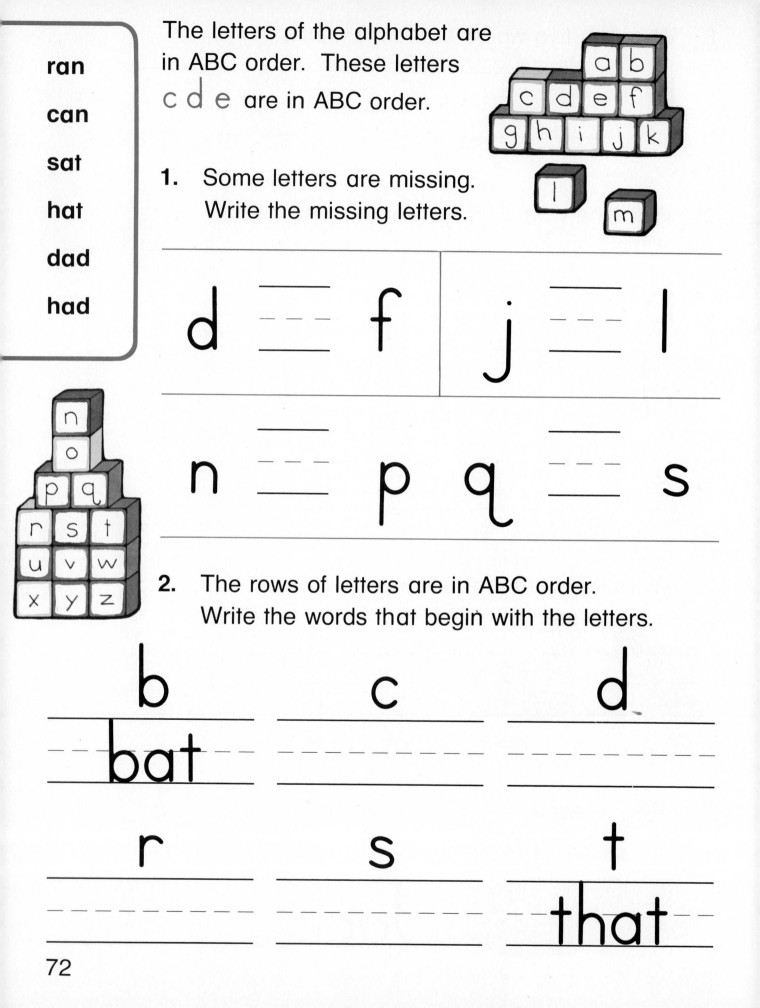

1. Some letters are missing. Write the missing letters.

d ___ f   j ___ l

n ___ p   q ___ s

2. The rows of letters are in ABC order. Write the words that begin with the letters.

b   c   d
bat

r   s   t
                      that

72

fat   cat   man   sad   and

A. Write the two words that tell about each picture.

1. _____   _____

2. _____   _____

B. Do these things.

_____

3. Write the word that starts with **m.**   _____

4. Take away the **m.**
   Write the word that is left.   _____

5. Add **d** at the end of the word.
   Write the new word.   _____

6. Add **h** at the beginning of the word.
   Write the new word.   _____

73

19

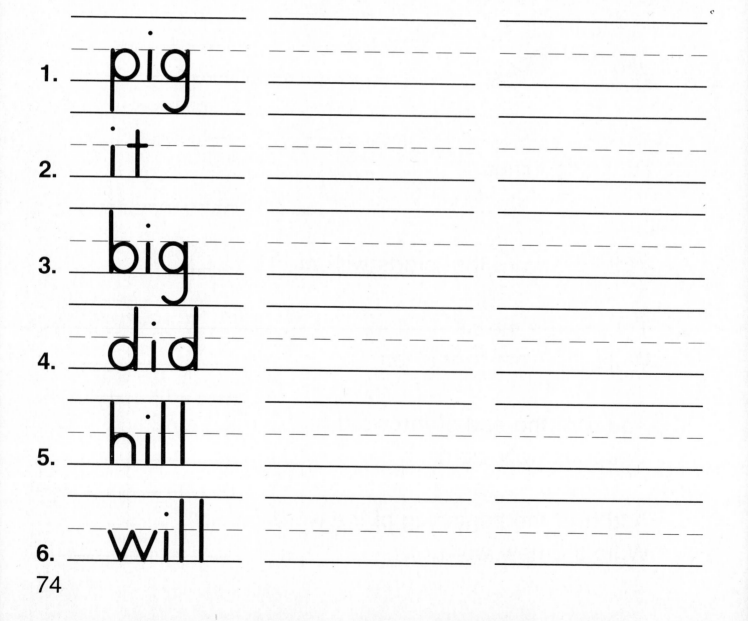

The letter **i** stands for the beginning sound in <u>it</u>. It stands for the middle sound in <u>pig</u>, too. Say the words. Listen for the sound of short **i.** Write each word two times.

1. pig
2. it
3. big
4. did
5. hill
6. will

74

1. Write the word that begins and ends
with the same letter.

_____

- - - - - - - - - -

_____

2. Write the two words that end like   .

_____   _____

- - - - - - - - - -   - - - - - - - - - -

_____   _____

3. Two words end with two letters that
are the same. Write the words.

_____   _____

- - - - - - - - - -   - - - - - - - - - -

_____   _____

4. Write the missing words. Use the same
word both times.

There is something in the box.

_____

- - - - - - - - - -

What is _____?

_____

- - - - - - - - - - -

I think _____ is a puppy.

5. Find the picture of the pig on page 153.
Write the word pig under the picture.

pig

it

big

did

hill

will

A. Make some new words. Say the picture word. Write the letter that stands for the beginning sound. Add the letter to i|| .

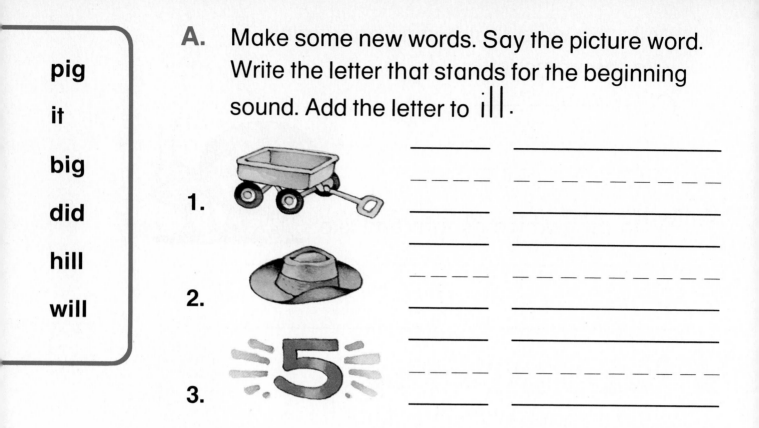

1.

2.

3.

B. Say these picture words. Write the letters that stand for the beginning sounds. Add the two letters to i|| .

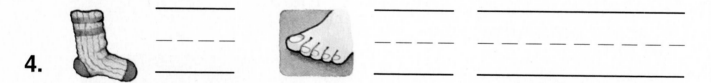

4.

C. Write the answer to the question. Use three of the words.

Who did it?

The

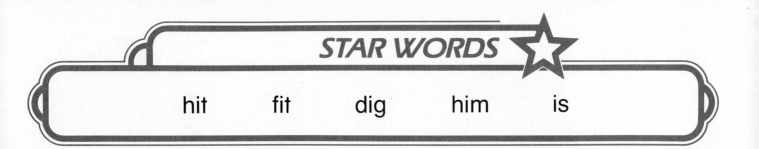

hit   fit   dig   him   is

Write the Star Words and some more words.

1. Write the word that has two letters.   ————————

2. Add **h** at the beginning.   ————————

3. Change **s** to **m.**   ————————

4. Change **m** to **t.**   ————————

5. Change **h** to **f.**   ————————

6. Change **t** to **g.**   ————————

7. Change **f** to **d.**   ————————

20

The sound at the beginning of <u>us</u> is spelled
with the letter **u.** You hear the same sound
in the middle of <u>but</u>.
Write each word two times.

1. bus

2. us

3. cut

4. but

5. fun

6. run

A. Write a word for each picture.
Then write a word that ends with
the same letter.

1. _____ _____

2. _____ _____

3. _____ _____

B. Change **a** to **u** in each word.
Write another word.

4. cat _____ **5.** ran _____

79

bus

us

cut

but

fun

run

Write the missing words.

_____

- - - - - - - - - -

1. Dad took _____ fishing.

_____

- - - - - - - - - -

2. We took the _____ to the river.

_____

- - - - - - - - - -

3. We had _____ walking on the rocks.

_____

- - - - - - - - - -

4. Dad told us not to _____.

_____

- - - - - - - - - -

5. I listened, _____ Josie did not.

_____

- - - - - - - - - -

6. She fell and _____ her hand.

nut   bug   sun   jump   duck

Write the word that fits with the others.

1. swan   goose   _____

2. moon   stars   _____

3. spider   ant   _____

4. walk   hop   _____

5. pine cone   acorn   _____

21

The middle sound in each word is spelled
with the letter **e.**
Say the words.
Write each word two times.

1. hen

2. wet

3. let

4. bed

5. get

6. yes

A. Words that rhyme sound the same at the end.

1. Write the three words that rhyme.

_____ _____ _____

2. Say the picture words.
Write words that rhyme with them.

 _____  _____

B. Write the letters and make a word.

3. Write the beginning letter in  . _____

4. Write the middle letter in . _____

5. Write the last letter in  . _____

6. Put the letters together.
Write the new word.

83

hen

wet

let

bed

get

yes

Stop is the opposite of go.

Up is the opposite of down.

A. Write the words that are the opposite.

1. dry _____

2. no _____

B. Write the missing words.

_____

3. Where did you _____ the eggs?

_____

4. I got them from the _____ .

_____

5. She _____ me take them.

84

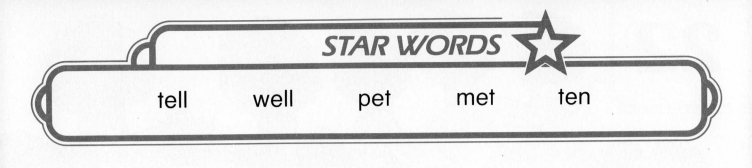
Here are some beginning letters.
Look at the dots under the letters.

f g m p t w

1. Find the letters with blue dots.
   Add each one to **ell.** Write three words.

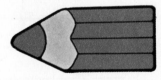

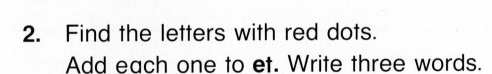

ell

2. Find the letters with red dots.
   Add each one to **et.** Write three words.

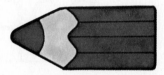

et

3. Find the letters with green dots.
   Add each one to **en.** Write three words.

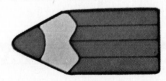

en

22

Listen to the sound in the middle of <u>hop</u> and <u>not</u>. The letter **o** spells that sound.
Say each word.
Write each word two times.

1. hop

2. stop

3. got

4. not

5. box

6. fox

1. Tell about the picture.
Write the missing words.

_____

_ _ _ _ _ _ _ _ _ _

The _____

_____

_ _ _ _ _ _ _ _ _ _

will _____ .

2. Write the words that tell about these pictures.

_____   _____

_ _ _ _ _ _ _ _ _ _   _ _ _ _ _ _ _ _ _ _

_____   _____

3. Write the two words that end with **t**.

_____   _____

_ _ _ _ _ _ _ _ _ _   _ _ _ _ _ _ _ _ _ _

_____   _____

4. Find the picture of a fox on page 149.
Write the word fox under the picture.

hop

stop

got

not

box

fox

Read the story about the fox and the rabbit.
Write the missing words.

The fox ran after the rabbit. The rabbit

_____

could _____ very fast. The fox

could not catch him.

The fox said, "I will catch him another way."

_____

So the fox _____ a box. He put

some food in the box. He said, "The rabbit will
stop to eat the food. I will catch him."

Soon the rabbit hopped by. He saw

_____

the food in the _____. He said,

_____

"The _____ put this here.

_____

I will not _____. The fox

_____

will _____ catch me."

spot	lot	top	pop	hot

1. Put the letters together to spell two words.

_____   _____

p t o   _____   _____

o t s p   _____   _____

2. Write three words that rhyme with <u>dot</u>.

_____   _____   _____

3. Write a word that begins and ends
with the same letter.

_____

4. Do you know another word that begins and
ends with the same letter?
Write it.

_____

89

Say the spelling words.
Spell each word.
Write each word two times.

UNIT 17

you

_____   _____
- - - - - - - - -   - - - - - - - - -
_____   _____

are
- - - - - - - - -   - - - - - - - - -
_____   _____

UNIT 18

_____   _____

can
- - - - - - - - -   - - - - - - - - -
_____   _____

had
- - - - - - - - -   - - - - - - - - -
_____   _____

UNIT 19

_____   _____

big
- - - - - - - - -   - - - - - - - - -
_____   _____

did
- - - - - - - - -   - - - - - - - - -
_____   _____

90

UNIT 17 What words sound like these letters?
Write the words.

1. u _____

2. r _____

UNIT 18 Write the missing words.

3. Tiggy _____
fish for dinner.

4. You _____ tell she liked it.

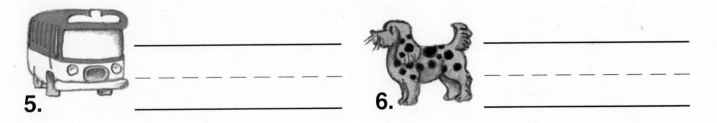

UNIT 19 Write the words that begin
with the same sounds.

5. _____

6. _____

UNITS 17–19 Write the words that begin with these letters.

7. a _____

8. b _____

9. c _____

10. d _____

Look at the words.
Each word has a vowel in the middle.
Write each word two times.

UNIT 20

run

but

UNIT 21

let

bed

UNIT 22

not

box

92

UNIT 20 Change the first letter. Write another word.

_____   _____
- - - - - - - - - - -   - - - - - - - - - - -
1. fun _____   2. cut _____

UNIT 21 Say the picture words.
Write the words that rhyme.

_____   _____
- - - - - - - - - - -   - - - - - - - - - - -
3. _____   4. _____

UNIT 22 Write the missing words.

_____   _____
- - - - - - - - - - -   - - - - - - - - - - -
5. Do _____ open this _____ .

UNITS 20 – 22 Write the missing words.

_____
- - - - - - - - - - -
6. Did your brother _____ in the race?

_____
- - - - - - - - - - -
7. Is it time to go to _____ ?

_____
- - - - - - - - - - -
8. This dog is _____ brown.

Say the spelling words.
Spell each word.
Write each word two times.

1. up

2. down

3. at

4. on

5. in

6. or

1. The letters **a, e, i, o,** and **u** are called vowels.
Write the words that begin with vowels.

_____   _____   _____

_ _ _ _ _ _ _ _ _ _   _ _ _ _ _ _ _ _ _ _   _ _ _ _ _ _ _ _ _ _

_____   _____   _____

_____   _____

_ _ _ _ _ _ _ _ _ _   _ _ _ _ _ _ _ _ _ _

_____   _____

2. Take away the first letter.
Write the word that is left.

_____   _____

_ _ _ _ _ _ _ _ _   _ _ _ _ _ _ _ _ _

sat _____   **for** _____

_____   _____

_ _ _ _ _ _ _ _ _   _ _ _ _ _ _ _ _ _

win _____   **cup** _____

3. Tell where the bear is going.
Write three words.

_____   _____   _____

_ _ _ _ _ _ _ _ _ _   _ _ _ _ _ _ _ _ _ _   _ _ _ _ _ _ _ _ _ _

_____   _____   _____

up

down

at

on

in

or

A. Write the word that tells where the cat is.

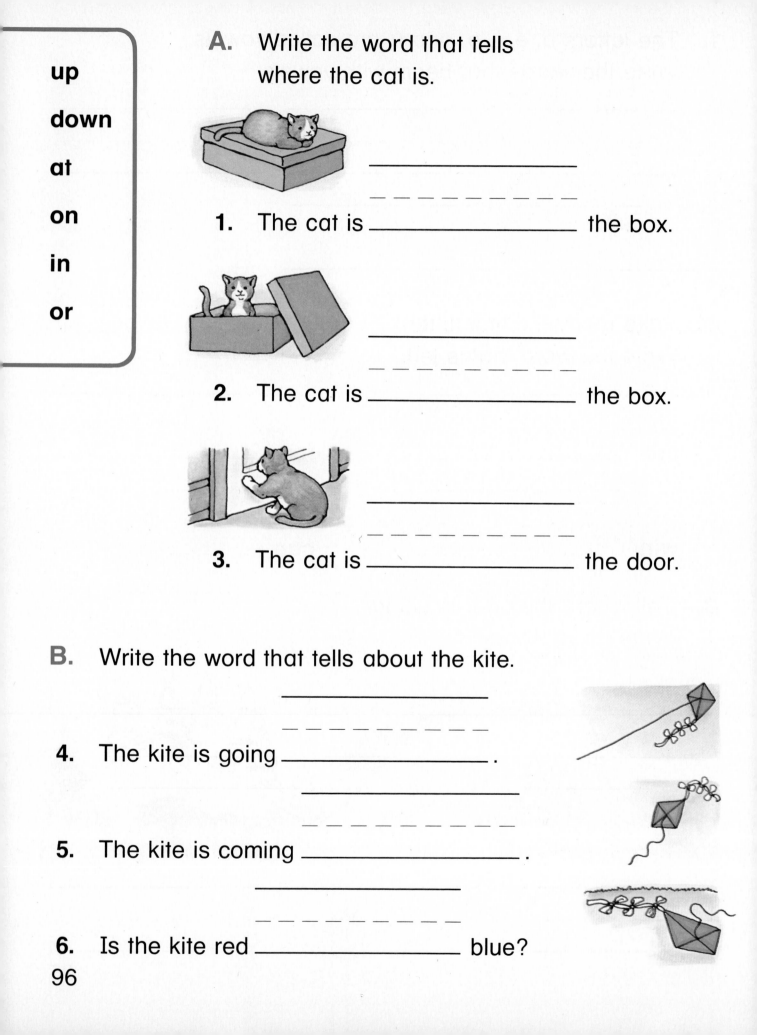

_____

- - - - - - - - - - - -

1. The cat is _____ the box.

2. The cat is _____ the box.

3. The cat is _____ the door.

B. Write the word that tells about the kite.

_____

- - - - - - - - - -

4. The kite is going _____ .

5. The kite is coming _____ .

6. Is the kite red _____ blue?

96

Tell about the pictures. Write the Star Words.

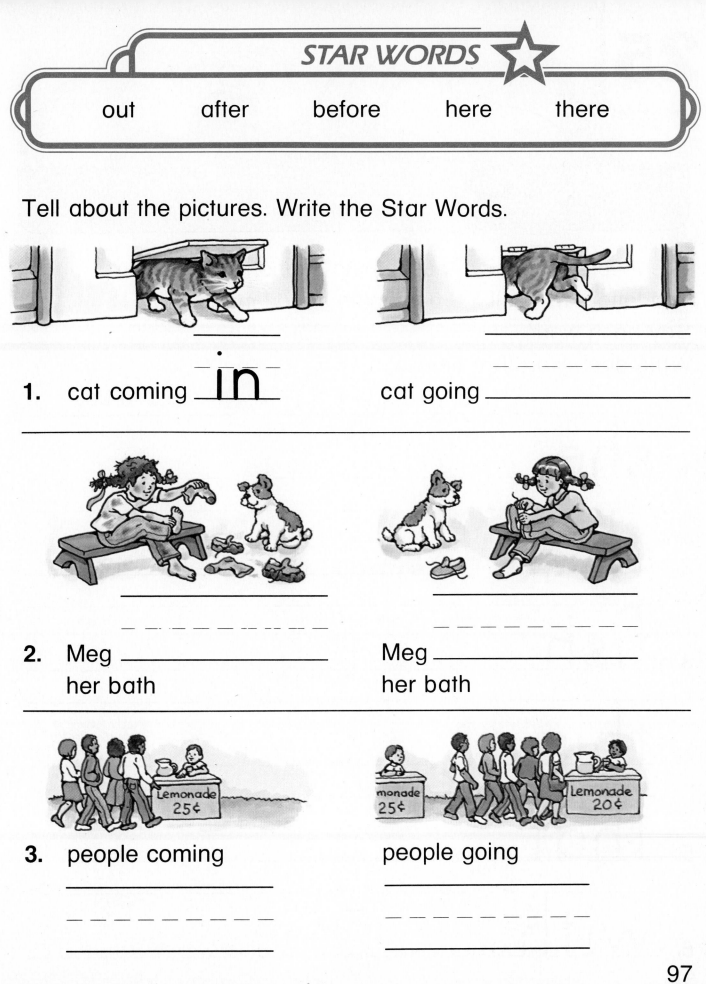

1. cat coming __in__   cat going _____

_____

2. Meg _____   Meg _____
    her bath   her bath

_____

3. people coming   people going

    _____   _____

The letters **sh** spell the beginning sound in <u>she</u>.
The letters **th** spell the beginning sound in <u>this</u>.
Say each word.
Write each word two times.

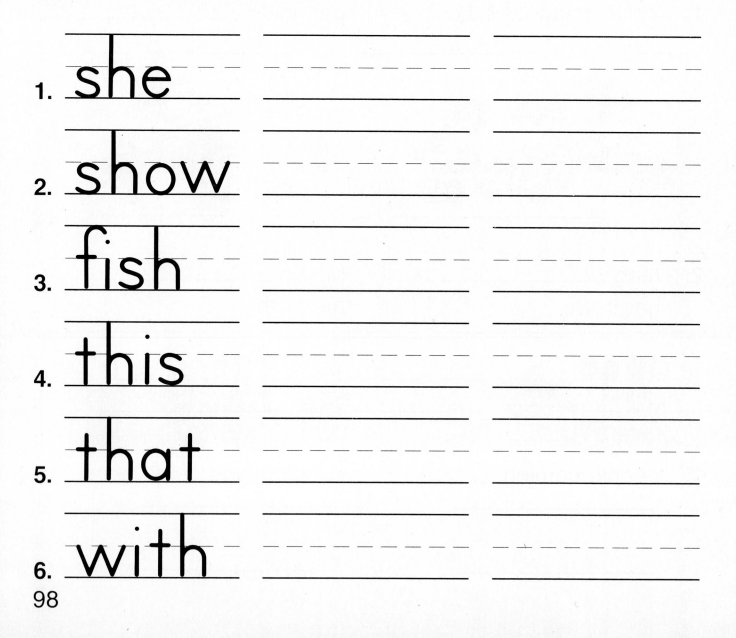

1. she

2. show

3. fish

4. this

5. that

6. with

1. Write the two words that begin with **th.**

_____   _____

_____   _____

2. Write the two words that begin with **sh.**

_____   _____

_____   _____

3. Write the two words that end with these letters.

th _____   sh _____

4. Write the missing words.

_____

a puppet _____

_____

a big _____

5. Find the picture of a fish on page 149.
Write the word fish under the picture.

she

show

fish

this

that

with

Write the missing words. Use each word once.

_____
- - - - - - - - - - - - - -

1. I went fishing _____ Grandpa.

_____
- - - - - - - - - - - - - -

2. We each got a _____ .

_____
- - - - - - - - - - - - - -

3. We went to _____ them to Grandma.

4. Grandpa said, "Guess which fish

_____
- - - - - - - - - - - - - -

_____ caught."

_____
- - - - - - - - - - - - - -

5. "Did she catch _____ little fish?"

_____
- - - - - - - - - - - - - -

6. "Or did she catch _____ big fish?"

| then | these | shut | shoe | wish |

Put the words together.
Write the sentences.

1. shut   First   eyes.   your

_____

- - - - - - - - - - - - - - - - -

_____

2. make   wish.   Then   a

_____

- - - - - - - - - - - - - - - - -

_____

3. We   fish.   these   got

_____

- - - - - - - - - - - - - - - - -

_____

4. this   old   got   we   Then   shoe.

_____

- - - - - - - - - - - - - - - - -

_____

_____

- - - - - - - - - - - - - - - - -

_____

101

26

Say the spelling words.
Spell each word.
Write each word two times.

1. baby

2. story

3. said

4. of

5. for

6. mother

A. Write two words each time.

1. They begin with **s.**

_____   _____

_____   _____

_____   _____

2. They have **f.**

_____   _____

_____   _____

_____   _____

3. They end with **y.**

_____   _____

_____   _____

_____   _____

B. Tell about the pictures.
Write the missing words.

_____

_____

4. _____ birds

_____

_____

5. _____ bird

baby

story

said

of

for

mother

Write <u>said</u>.
Then write the answer.

Why is the baby crying?

The baby wants his mother.

1. He ____ , " ____

____

____ . "

____ .

What story do you like?

We like the story of Peter Pan.

2. They ____ .

" ____

____ "

____ .

104

Write the missing words.

_____

- - - - - - - -

1. I have a _____ book.

_____

- - - - - - - -

2. It is _____ turtles.

_____

- - - - - - - -

3. Baby turtles _____ from eggs.

_____

- - - - - - - -

4. Here is a picture of _____ baby turtles.

_____

- - - - - - - -

5. I _____ it is fun to learn about animals.

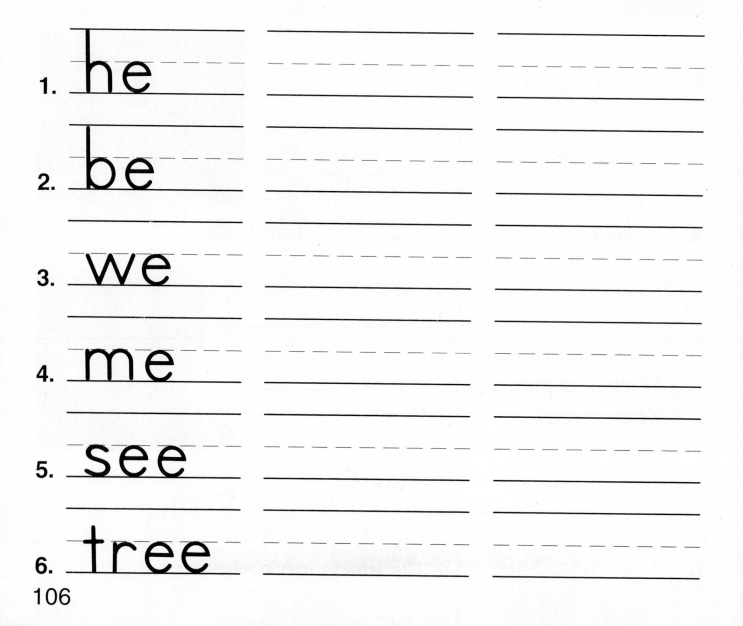

27

Listen to the sound at the end
of <u>he</u>. It is like the name for **e**.
You can spell this sound with **e** or **ee**.
Say each word.
Write each word two times.

1. he

2. be

3. we

4. me

5. see

6. tree

1. Look at the picture sentence.
Write the words.

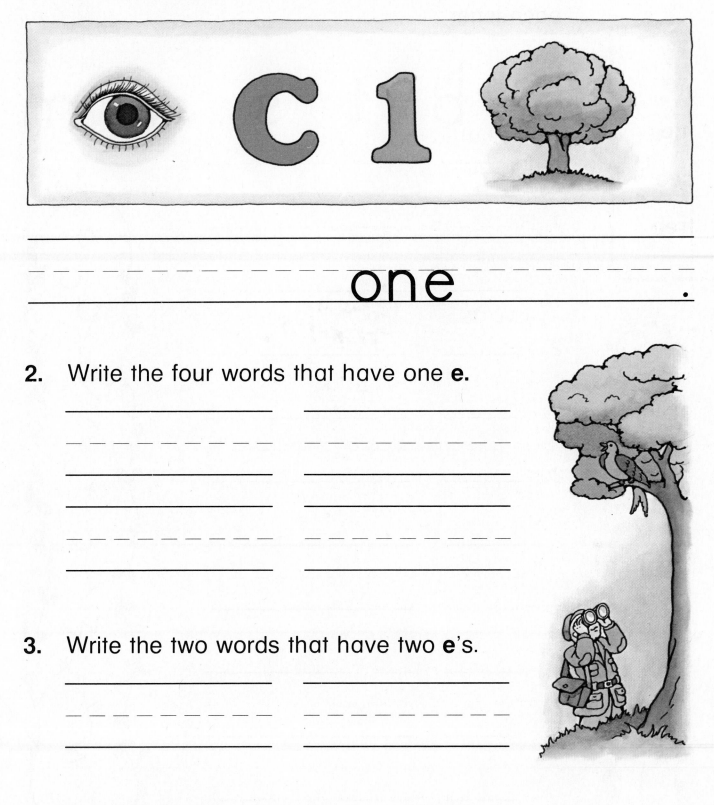

one   .

2. Write the four words that have one **e.**

_____   _____

_____   _____

3. Write the two words that have two **e**'s.

_____   _____

4. Find the picture of a tree on page 156.
Write the word tree under the picture.

he

be

we

me

see

tree

Write these letters in ABC order.
Then write the word that starts with
each letter.

h   b   t   s   w   m

_____ _____

1. _____ _____

2. _____ _____

3. _____ _____

4. _____ _____

5. _____ _____

6. _____ _____

bee   free   three   deep   seed

A.   What words are missing?
Write the words below.

Amy's cat had __1__ kittens.
Amy must give the kittens away.
Would you like a __2__ kitten?

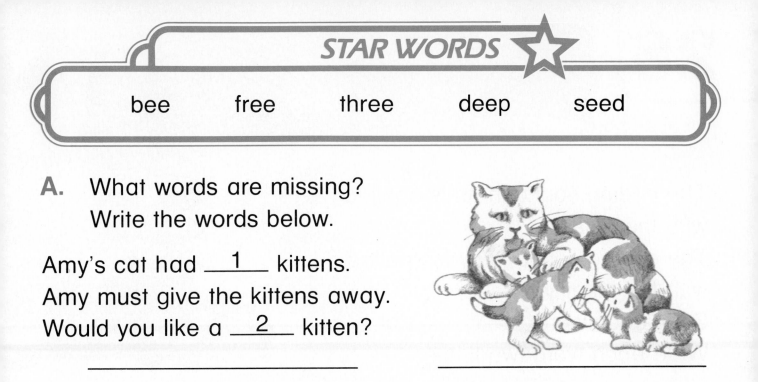

_____   _____

- - - - - - - - - - - - - -   - - - - - - - - - - - - - -

1. _____   **2.** _____

Mike planted a flower __3__.
A bird came and ate it.
The seed was not __4__ enough.

_____   _____

- - - - - - - - - - - - - -   - - - - - - - - - - - - - -

3. _____   **4.** _____

B.   Do not mix up <u>be</u> and <u>bee</u>. You use <u>be</u> to say:
"Be careful." The word <u>bee</u> names this:  .
Write the right word.

_____

- - - - - - - - -

5. Do not _____ afraid.

_____

- - - - - - - - -

6. The _____ will fly away.

109

28

The ending sound in <u>go</u> is spelled
with the letter **o.**
The ending sound in <u>fly</u> is spelled
with the letter **y.**
Spell each word.
Write each word two times.

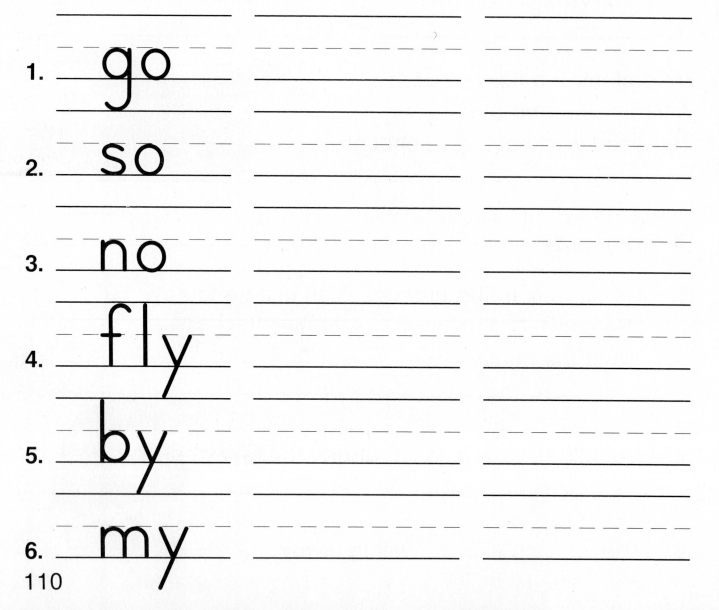

1. go

2. so

3. no

4. fly

5. by

6. my

A. Write the words.

1. Say the name for the letter **o**.
What words have this sound?

_____   _____   _____

2. Say the name for the letter **i**.
What words have this sound?

_____   _____   _____

B. Add **o** or **y**. Write the words.

3. b _____   **4.** g _____

5. n _____   **6.** fl _____

7. s _____   **8.** m _____

go
so
no
fly
by
my

Put the words in order.
Write sentences.

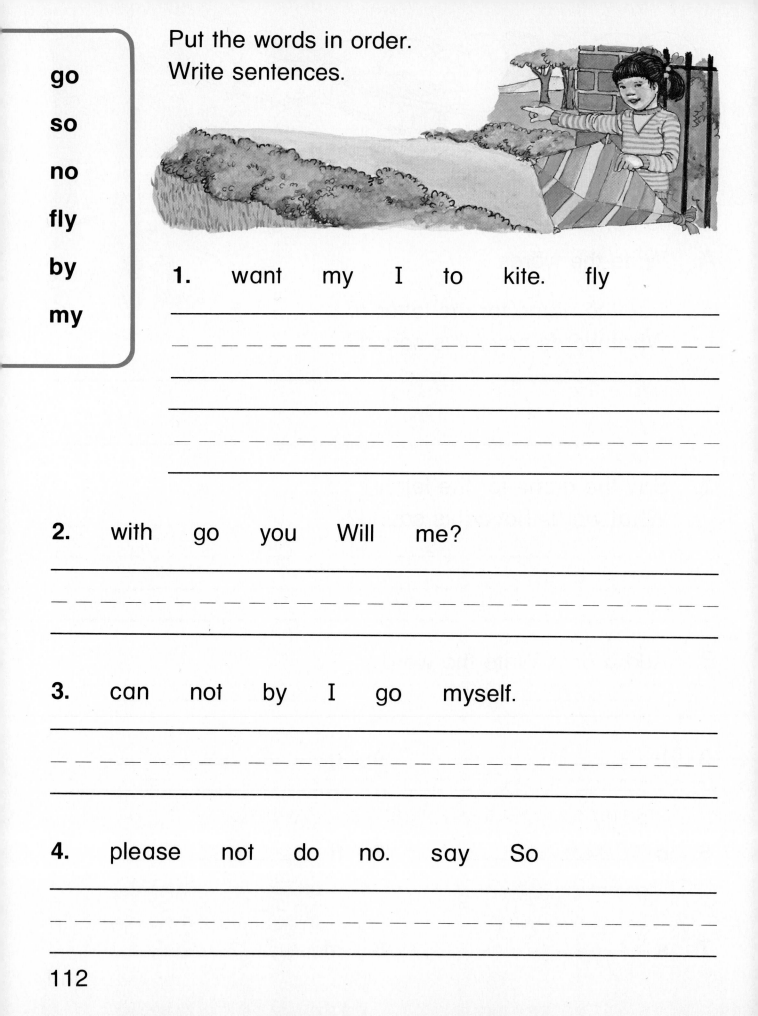

1. want   my   I   to   kite.   fly

_____

- - - - - - - - - - - - - - - - - - -

_____

- - - - - - - - - - - - - - - - - - -

_____

2. with   go   you   Will   me?

_____

- - - - - - - - - - - - - - - - - - -

_____

3. can   not   by   I   go   myself.

_____

- - - - - - - - - - - - - - - - - - -

_____

4. please   not   do   no.   say   So

_____

- - - - - - - - - - - - - - - - - - -

_____

to   do   try   cry   sky

The letters of the alphabet are in ABC order.
Words can be in ABC order, too. <u>Cat</u>, <u>dog</u>,
<u>elephant</u> are in ABC order.

A.   Write the words in ABC order.

1. by
do
cry

2. run
to
sky

3. try
fly
sky

_____   _____   _____

_____   _____   _____

_____   _____   _____

_____   _____   _____

B.   Add **ry** to each letter. Write three words.
Are the words in ABC order?

4. __c_____   **5.** __d_____   **6.** __t_____

Say the spelling words.
Spell each word.
Write each word two times.

UNIT 24

on

down

UNIT 25

she

that

UNIT 26

mother

for

UNIT 24 Write the missing words.

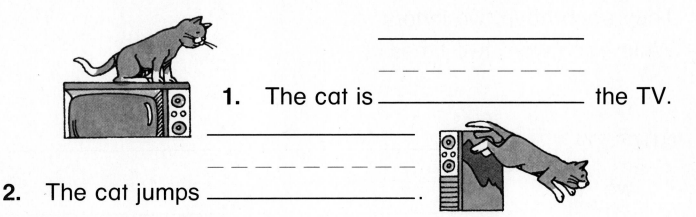

1. The cat is ——————————— the TV.

2. The cat jumps ——————————— .

UNIT 25 Tell about the pictures.
Write the missing words.

3.   this hat

                                        hat

4.   he sings

                                        sings

UNIT 26 Write the missing words.

5. The flowers are

——————————— ——————————— my ——————————— .

Look at the words.
They each have two letters.
Write each word two times.

UNIT 27

we

_____ _____

_____ _____

me

_____ _____

UNIT 28

go

_____ _____

_____ _____

my

_____ _____

116

UNIT 27 Say the picture word.
Write the words that rhyme.

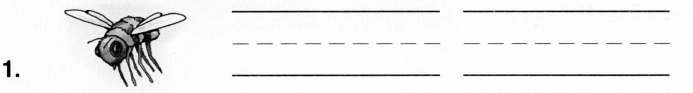

1. _____   _____
   - - - - - - - - - - -   - - - - - - - - - - -
   _____   _____

UNIT 28 Say the picture words.
Write words that begin with the same sounds.

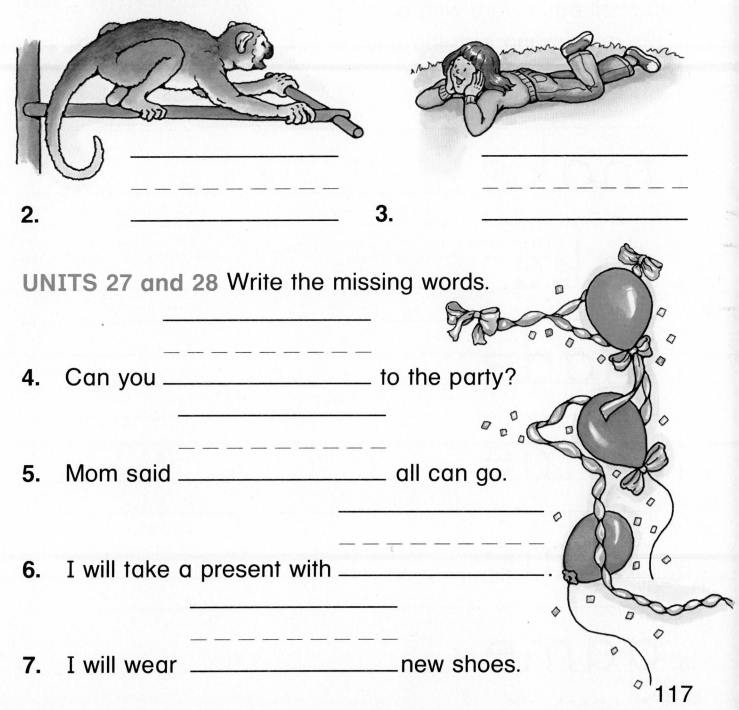

2. _____

3. _____

UNITS 27 and 28 Write the missing words.

_____
- - - - - - - - - -

4. Can you _____ to the party?

_____
- - - - - - - - - -

5. Mom said _____ all can go.

_____
- - - - - - - - - -

6. I will take a present with _____.

_____
- - - - - - - - - -

7. I will wear _____ new shoes.

117

Say the name for the letter **a**.
This sound is long **a**. Say the
words. Listen for long **a**.
You spell each word with **a**
in the middle and **e** at the end.
Write each word two times.

1. make _____ _____

2. take _____ _____

3. made _____ _____

4. came _____ _____

5. name _____ _____

6. game _____ _____

A. Write the missing letters.

1. c ___ m
2. g ___ m
3. m ___ k
4. m ___ d
5. n ___ m
6. t ___ k

B. Each sign stands for a letter.

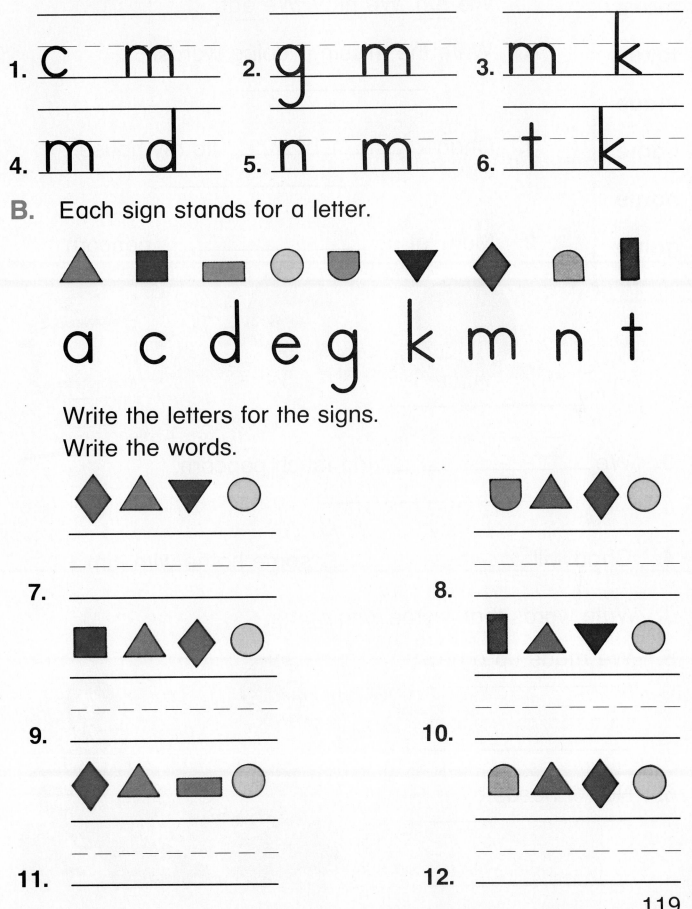

a   c   d   e   g   k   m   n   t

Write the letters for the signs.
Write the words.

7. _____

8. _____

9. _____

10. _____

11. _____

12. _____

119

make

take

made

came

name

game

Some words tell what we do.
We <u>run</u>. We <u>play</u>. We <u>eat</u>.

A. Write the missing "doing words."

_____

1. Chad _____ to my house.

_____

2. Mom let us _____ popcorn.

3. We _____ too much popcorn.

4. Chad will _____ some home with him.

B. Write words that rhyme with <u>came</u>.

5. We made up a new
_____
_____ .

6. Now it needs a
_____
_____ .

Finish the words.
First write the beginning letter
of the picture word.
Find another letter in the picture.
Write that letter next.

Then write the whole word.

c a m e

1. a e

2. a e

3. a e

4. a e

5. a e

31

The first three words have **i** in the middle.

The last three words have **o** in the middle.

All of the words end with **e**.

Read the words.

Write each word two times.

1. ride

2. like

3. five

4. rope

5. home

6. nose

1. Add the missing letters i and e.

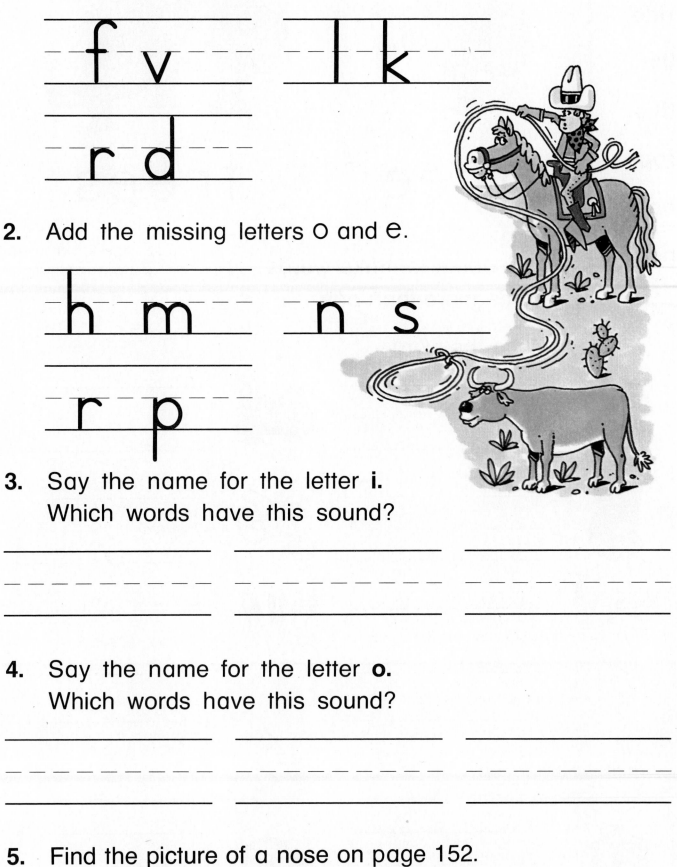

f v   l k

r d

2. Add the missing letters o and e.

h m   n s

r p

3. Say the name for the letter **i.**
Which words have this sound?

_____   _____   _____

_____   _____   _____

4. Say the name for the letter **o.**
Which words have this sound?

_____   _____   _____

_____   _____   _____

5. Find the picture of a nose on page 152.
Write the word nose under the picture.

ride

like

five

rope

home

nose

tree   trees

You add **s** to make words
name more than one.

Write the words.

124

time   side   bike   those   hope

Write the missing words.
Make some words name more than one.

1. This _____ is red.

2. But _____ _____ are blue.

3. One _____ is yellow.

4. Two _____ are green.

5. What _____ is it?

6. I _____ I am not late.

125

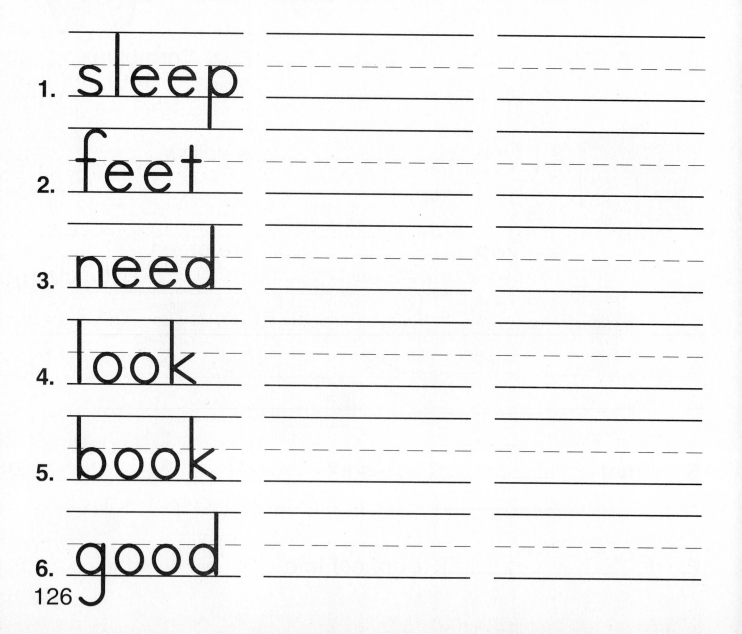

32

Look at the words.
Each word has two vowel letters
that are the same. They are **ee** or **oo**.
Say the words.
Write each word two times.

1. sleep

2. feet

3. need

4. look

5. book

6. good

A. Write the words that end with these letters.

1. d _____ _____

2. k _____ _____

B. Write the picture words.

3. _____

4. _____

5. _____

6. _____

C. Change the red letter.
Write one of your words.

7. seed 8. meet 9. steep

_____ _____ _____

127

sleep

feet

need

look

book

good

A. Answer the questions.

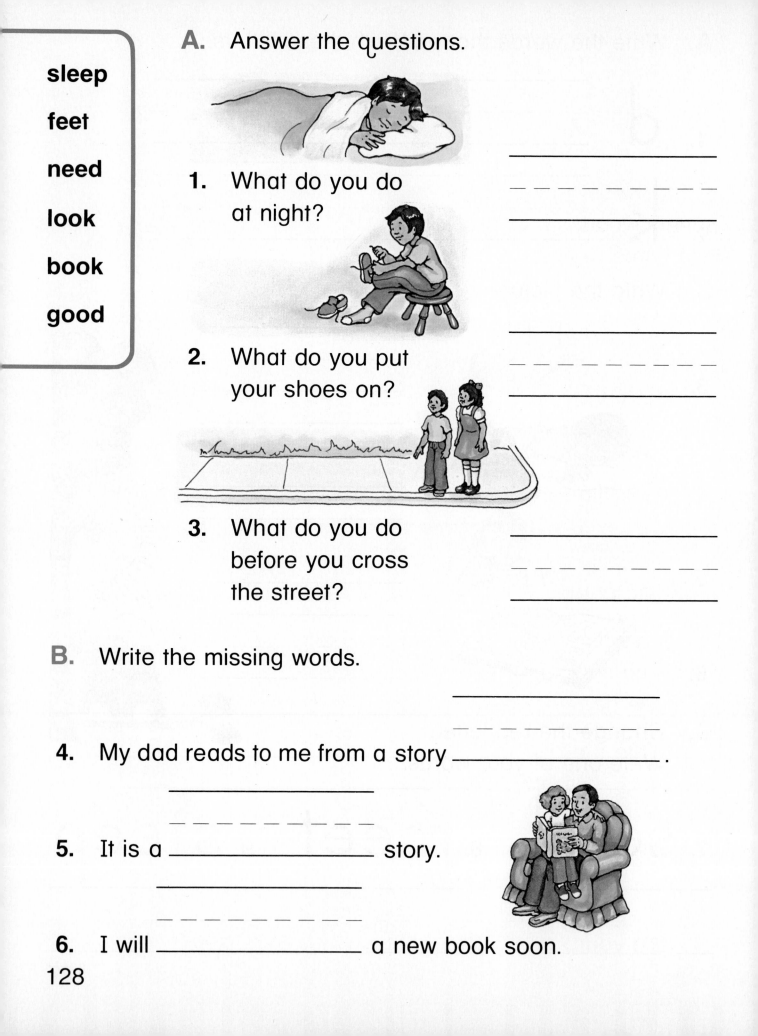

1. What do you do
   at night?

   _____
   - - - - - - - - -
   _____

2. What do you put
   your shoes on?

   _____
   - - - - - - - - -
   _____

3. What do you do
   before you cross
   the street?

   _____
   - - - - - - - - -
   _____

B. Write the missing words.

_____
- - - - - - - - -

4. My dad reads to me from a story _____ .

_____
- - - - - - - - -

5. It is a _____ story.

_____
- - - - - - - - -

6. I will _____ a new book soon.

128

street	sheep	feel	cook	wood

Some words name things.
Sheep, wood, street are words
that name things.

A. Write the missing "naming words."

_____

_ _ _ _ _ _ _ _

1. Did you pet the _____?

_____

_ _ _ _ _ _ _ _

2. Look before you cross the _____.

_____

_ _ _ _ _ _ _ _

3. Dad put _____ on the fire.

Other words tell things we do.
Feel and cook are words that tell
what we do.

B. Write the missing "doing words."

_____

_ _ _ _ _ _ _ _

4. Jake wanted to _____ the water.

_____

_ _ _ _ _ _ _ _

5. Did your sister _____ the dinner?

129

Look at the words.
Each word has two vowels
ea, ai, or **oa.**
Spell each word.
Write each word two times.

1. rain

2. wait

3. eat

4. clean

5. coat

6. boat

1. Write the picture words.

_____
_ _ _ _ _ _ _ _ _
_____

_____
_ _ _ _ _ _ _ _ _
_____

2. Put the words together to make a new word.

_____
_ _ _ _ _ _ _ _ _ _ _ _ _ _
_____

3. Write the picture words.

_____
_ _ _ _ _ _ _ _ _
_____

_____
_ _ _ _ _ _ _ _ _
_____

_____
_ _ _ _ _ _ _ _ _
_____

_____
_ _ _ _ _ _ _ _ _
_____

4. Find the picture of a boat on page 146.
Write the word boat under the picture.

| rain |
| wait |
| eat |
| clean |
| coat |
| boat |

The letters of the alphabet are in ABC order.
These letters are in ABC order def.
Words can be in ABC order, too.
Apple, bed, came are in ABC order.

A. The words are in ABC order. Write <u>eat</u>,
<u>coat</u>, and <u>boat</u> in the right places.

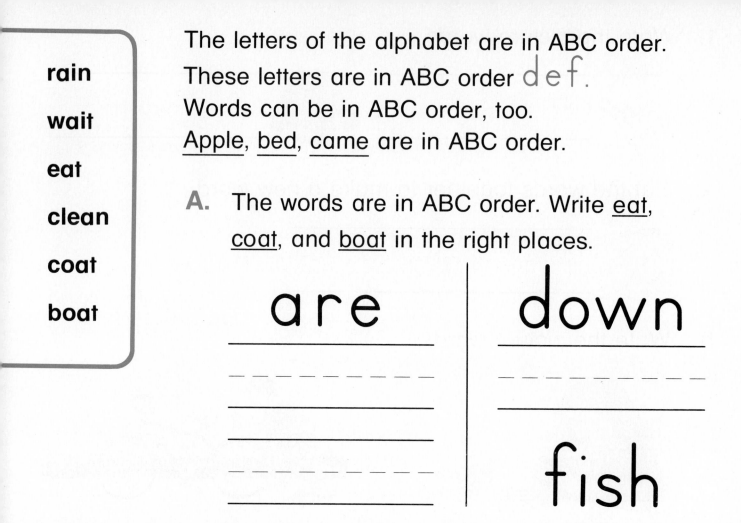

a r e

down

fish

B. There is something wrong with one word in
each sentence. Draw a line under the word.
Write it the right way.

1. I do not like the ran.

2. We had to wat for the bus.

3. My clen boots got muddy.

132

goat   train   paint   head   neat

A. Write the words for three things in the picture.

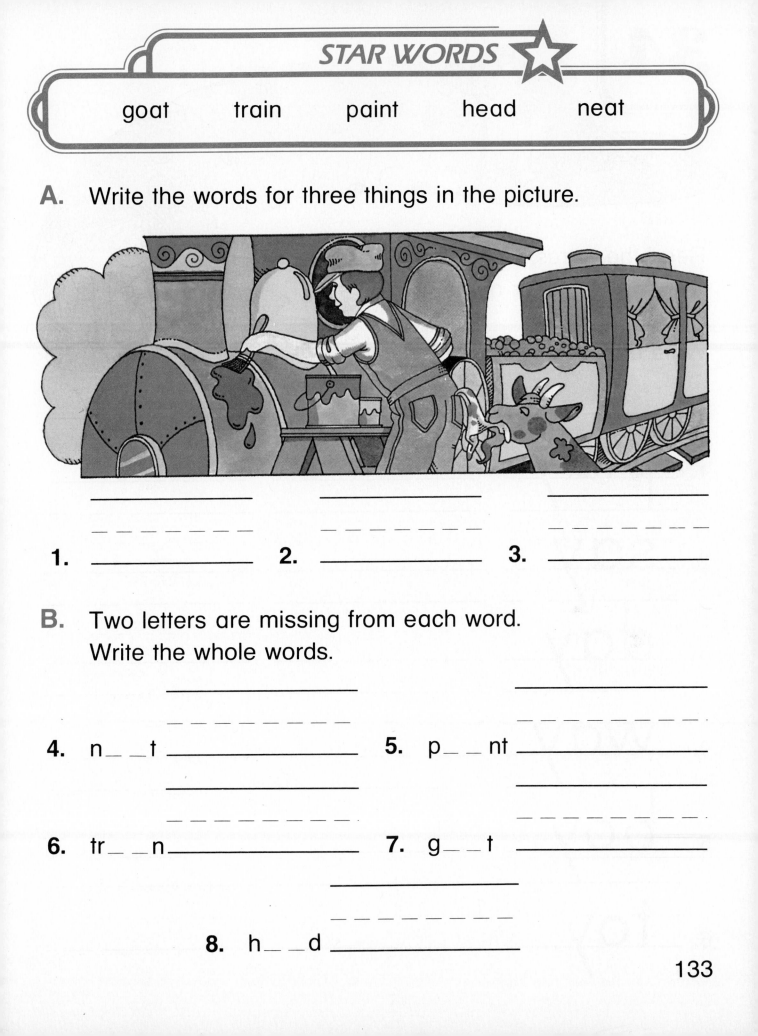

1. _____ 2. _____ 3. _____

B. Two letters are missing from each word.
Write the whole words.

4. n _ _ t _____ 5. p _ _ nt _____

6. tr _ _ n _____ 7. g _ _ t _____

8. h _ _ d _____

133

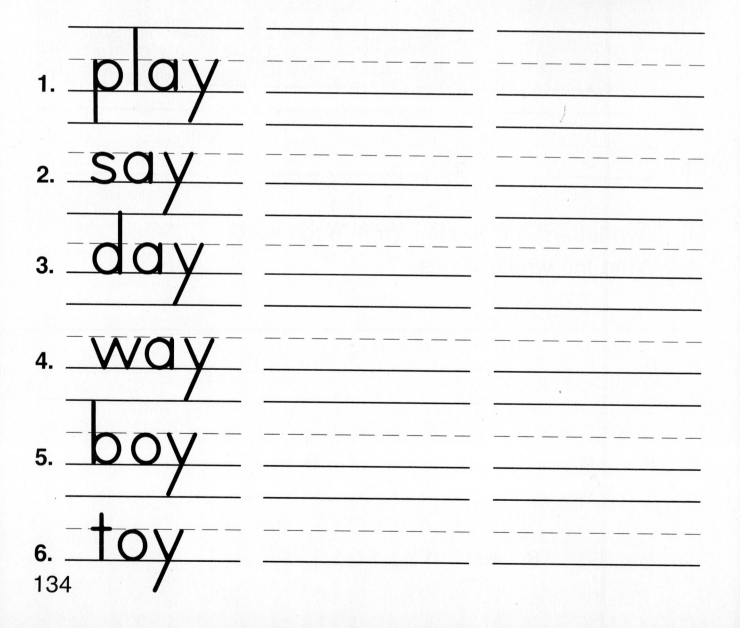

34

Read the words. Each word ends
with a vowel letter and **y.**
Spell each word.
Write each word two times.

1. play _____ _____

2. say _____ _____

3. day _____ _____

4. way _____ _____

5. boy _____ _____

6. toy _____ _____

134

1. Write the four words that rhyme.

_____ _____

_____ _____

2. Write the picture words.

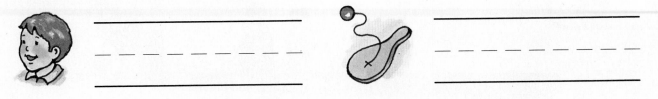

_____ _____

3. Write say, toy, day, and boy. Put them in ABC order with these words.

_____

coat

rain

4. Find the picture of a boy on page 147. Write the word boy under the picture.

135

play

say

day

way

boy

toy

You add **s** to make words name more than one.

toy

toys

A. Add **s** to naming words.

1. There are seven _____ in a week.

2. There are three _____ in line.

3. There are two _____ to jump rope.

B. Write the action words.

4. What did Dad _____?

5. He said we could _____.

136

joy	may	stay	away	says

A. Write the words that begin with
the missing letters.

b c d e f

g h i ⬚ k l

⬚ n o p q r

⬚ t u v w x y z

_____

_____

_____

_____

_____

B. Write the missing words.

_____

1. This animal _____ "Rib-it."

_____

2. Then it hops _____. What is it?

137

Say the spelling words.
Spell each word.
Write each word two times.

1. car

2. saw

3. one

4. all

5. little

6. children

1. Write the words for the pictures.

_____
_ _ _ _ _ _ _ _ _ _
_____

_____
_ _ _ _ _ _ _ _ _ _
_____

_____
_ _ _ _ _ _ _ _ _ _
_____

2. Write the word that is the opposite.

big

_____
_ _ _ _ _ _ _ _ _ _
_____

3. Write the words that have an **a.**

_____ _____ _____
_ _ _ _ _   _ _ _ _ _   _ _ _ _ _
_____ _____ _____

4. Find the picture of a car on page 147.
Write the word car under the picture.

Write the missing words.

car

saw

one

all

little

children

_____

- - - - - - - - - - -

1. The _____
   went to the circus.

_____

- - - - - - - - -

2. They _____ the clowns.

_____

- - - - - - - - -

3. The clowns rode in a red _____ .

4. The car was very

_____

- - - - - - - -

_____ .

5. The clowns were

_____

- - - - - - -

_____ inside.

_____

- - - - - - - -

6. There were three clowns and _____ dog.

140

every   want   work   school   what

A. Write three words that begin with **w.**

_____   _____   _____

1. _____   **2.** _____   **3.** _____

B. Write the missing words.

_____

4. Tina is going to _____.

5. Tina's mother is going to

_____

_____.

6. They leave together

_____

_____ morning.

7. Can you tell

_____

_____ Tina's mother does?

36 REVIEW

Say the spelling words.
Spell each word.
Write each word two times.

UNIT 30

make

came

UNIT 31

like

home

UNIT 32

sleep

good

142

UNIT 30 Say the picture words.
Write the words that rhyme.

 1. _____

 2. _____

UNIT 31 Change the red letter.
Write one of your words.

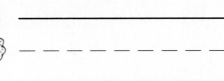

3. **lake** _____

4. **hole** _____

UNIT 32 Write the words that end
with the same sound.

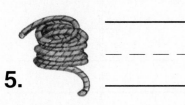 5. _____

 6. _____

UNITS 30–32 Write the words that have a vowel letter
in the middle and an **e** at the end.

7. _____

8. _____

9. _____

10. _____

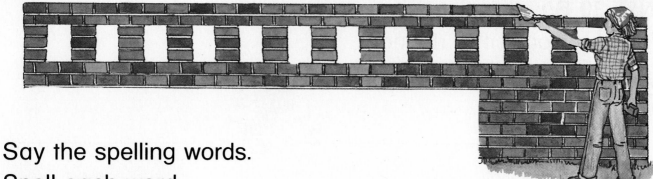

Say the spelling words.
Spell each word.
Write each word two times.

UNIT 33

eat

_____   _____
_ _ _ _ _ _ _ _ _ _ _ _   _ _ _ _ _ _ _ _ _ _ _ _
_____   _____

boat

_ _ _ _ _ _ _ _ _ _ _ _   _ _ _ _ _ _ _ _ _ _ _ _
_____   _____

UNIT 34

play

_____   _____
_ _ _ _ _ _ _ _ _ _ _ _   _ _ _ _ _ _ _ _ _ _ _ _
_____   _____

boy

_ _ _ _ _ _ _ _ _ _ _ _   _ _ _ _ _ _ _ _ _ _ _ _
_____   _____

UNIT 35

little

_____   _____
_ _ _ _ _ _ _ _ _ _ _ _   _ _ _ _ _ _ _ _ _ _ _ _
_____   _____

saw

_ _ _ _ _ _ _ _ _ _ _ _   _ _ _ _ _ _ _ _ _ _ _ _
_____   _____

UNIT 33 Write the missing words.

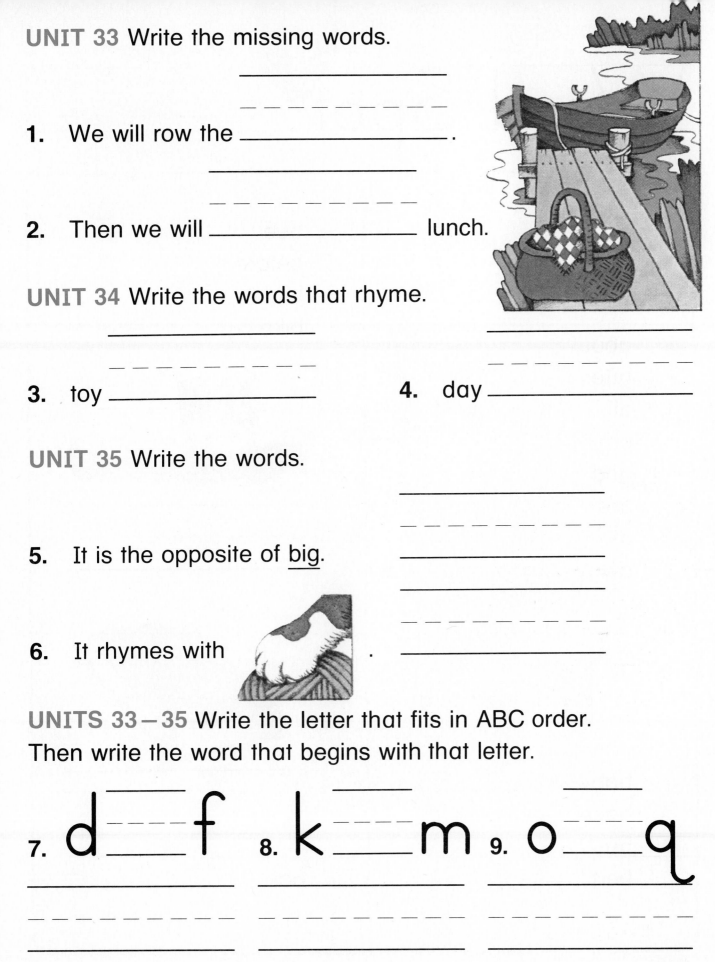

_____

__ __ __ __ __ __

1. We will row the _____ .

_____

__ __ __ __ __ __

2. Then we will _____ lunch.

UNIT 34 Write the words that rhyme.

_____   _____

__ __ __ __ __ __   __ __ __ __ __ __

3. toy _____   4. day _____

UNIT 35 Write the words.

_____

__ __ __ __ __ __

_____

5. It is the opposite of big.   _____

__ __ __ __ __ __

6. It rhymes with [image] . _____

UNITS 33 – 35 Write the letter that fits in ABC order.
Then write the word that begins with that letter.

7. d __ f   8. k __ m   9. o __ q

_____   _____   _____

__ __ __ __   __ __ __ __   __ __ __ __

Word Spot

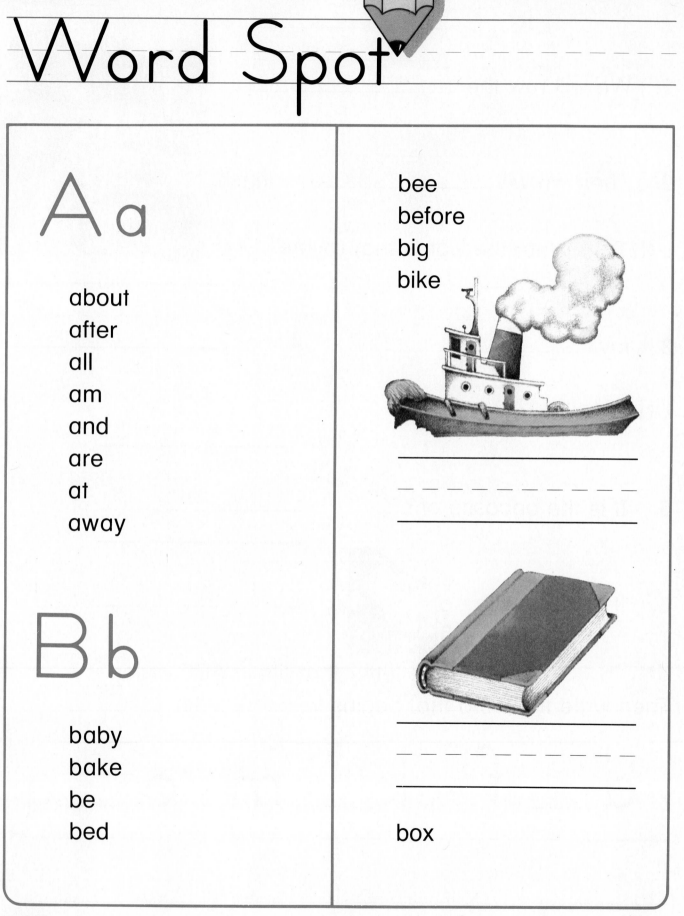

Aa

about
after
all
am
and
are
at
away

Bb

baby
bake
be
bed

bee
before
big
bike

_____

- - - - - - - - - -

_____

_____

- - - - - - - - - -

_____

box

bug
bus
but
by

Cc

cake
came
can

cat
children
clean

come
cook
cry
cut

D d

dad
day
deep
did
dig
do

_____

down

E e

eat
every

F f

face
fat
feel

G

Gg

fit
five
fly
for

free
fun

get
go

good
got

Hh

had
has
hat
have
he
head

here
hill
him
hit

home

hot

I i

I
in
is
it

J j

joy
jump

K k

L l

let
like
little
look
lot

M m

made
make

may
me
met

my

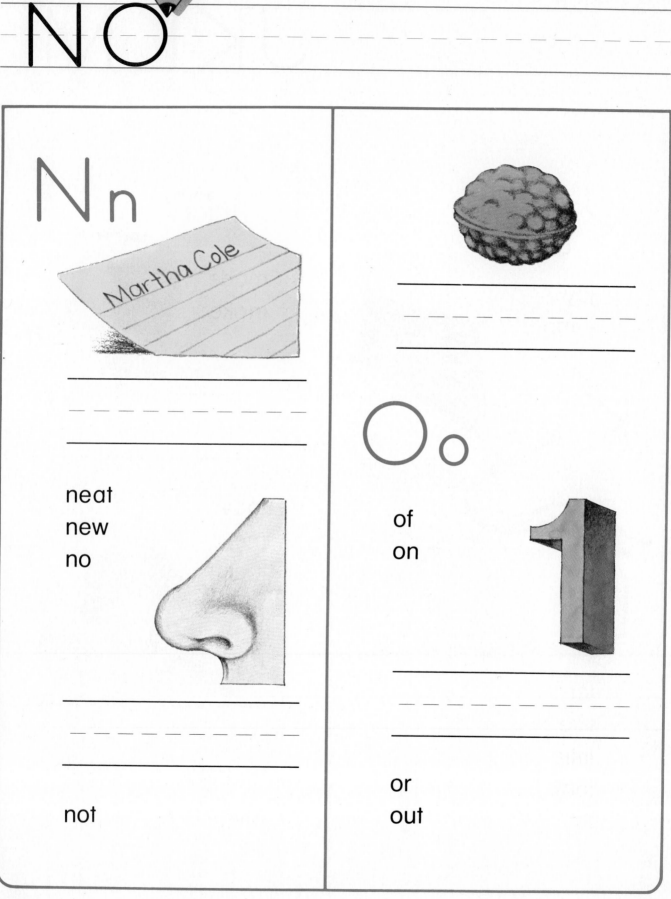

N n

Martha Cole

neat
new
no

not

O o

of
on

or
out

PQR

Pp

pet

play
pop

Qq

Rr

race
rain
ride

run

S s

said
same
sat
saw
say
says

see

seed
she
sheep

show
shut
side
sky

so

some
spot
stay
stop
story
street

T t

take
tell

10

that
the
then
there
they
think
this
those
three

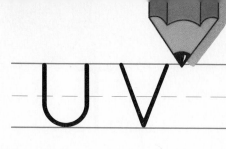

U V

to
top

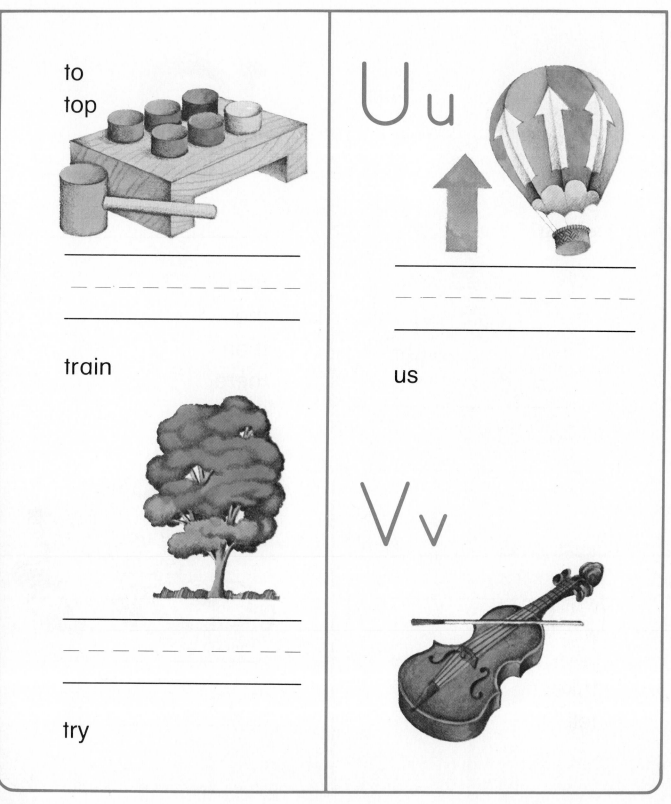

train

try

Uu

us

Vv

W w

wait
want
was
way
well
were

_____

- - - - - - - -

_____

what
will
wish
wood
work

X x

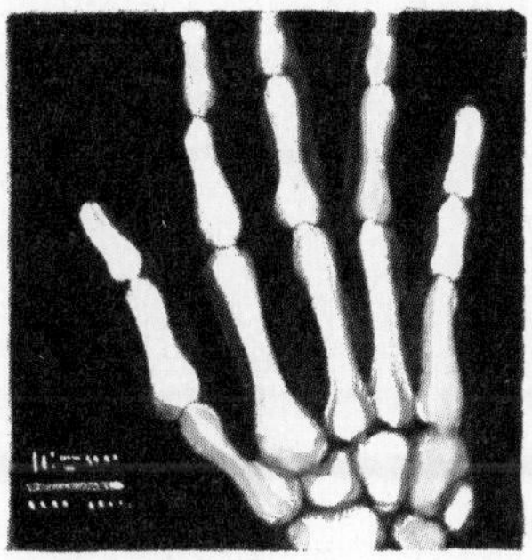

Y y

yes
yet

Z z

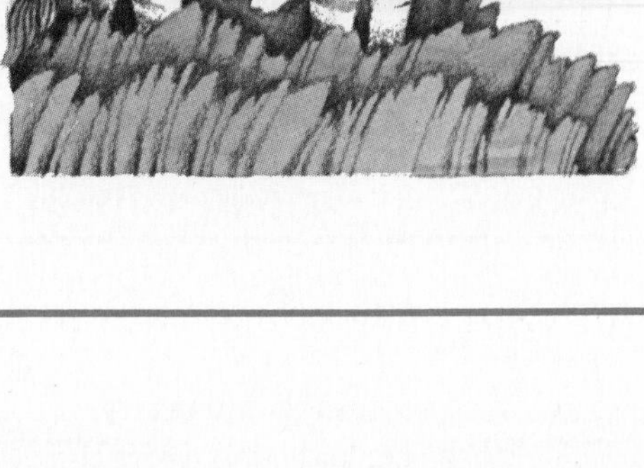